Anna Hicks

Just One More Day

Meditations for Those Who Struggle with Anxiety and Depression

Beverlee Buller Keck

Winnipeg, MB

KINDRED
PRODUCTIONS

Goessel, KS

Published simultaneously by Kindred Productions, Winnipeg, Manitoba R3M 3Z6 and Kindred Productions, Goessel, Kansas 67053

Scripture taken from the NEW AMERICAN STANDARD BIBLE®, Copyright © 1960,1962,1963,1968,1971,1972,1973,1975,1977,1995 by The Lockman Foundation. Used by permission.

Unless otherwise indicated, all other Scripture quotations are taken from the Holy Bible, New Living Translation, copyright 1996, 2004. Used by permission of Tyndale House Publishers, Inc., Wheaton, Illinois 60189. All rights reserved.

Cover and Book Design: Fred Koop
Printed by Friesens

Library and Archives Canada Cataloguing in Publication

Keck, Beverlee Buller, 1953-
    Just one more day : meditations for those who struggle with anxiety and depression / Beverlee Buller Keck.

Includes bibliographical references.
ISBN 978-1-894791-21-2

    1. Keck, Beverlee Buller, 1953- --Mental health.
2. Anxiety--Religious aspects--Christianity. 3. Depression, Mental--Religious aspects--Christianity. 4. Meditations.
5. Depressed persons--Biography. I. Title.

BV4910.34.K43 2009   248.8'625   C2009-904390-4

Visit our website at www.kindredproductions.com
Printed in Canada

Contents

This book is dedicated to my late father,

Walter John Buller,

who inspired me to pursue writing.

He always had a dream to publish a book.

He would be so proud of this accomplishment.

Thanks, Dad!

Acknowledgments

I have relished the opportunity to identify the people who have influenced my writing. I've always wondered what it would be like to author a book and be able to write this page. (Writing this page means I have written a book!)

First, I would like to thank Kindred Productions and its staff for seeing this project through. I hope Kindred Productions takes consolation in the fact that those who struggle with anxiety and depression will, I hope, receive some encouragement and guidance through this book.

I have benefited from the professional treatment of Dr. Ronald G. Carlson and Dr. Glenn E. McClellan. Many of the concepts I learned from them are embedded in these pages.

I would like to thank Dr. Doug Geivett and Dr. Gregory E. Ganssle for their professional writing consultations. I also want to acknowledge the professional services of Ellsworth Vines, Clint McCord, Susan Miller, Linda Manassee Buell and Jason Armstrong.

I would like to thank Nancy Fielder for her sacrificial time digging her way through the entries, employing her grammatical skills before Kindred Productions went through it. Nancy was not only an editorial aide but also a friend who delivered an abundance of meals during a particularly difficult season. Her generosity is something that has meant so much to me.

Others have also had a profound impact on my journey. My husband, Durwin, worked faithfully and tirelessly through the painful days of the last several years. I hope my daughter, Molly, will inherit some blessings from this project. Charles Buller, my brother, has been a benefactor in profound ways throughout my adult years and a sacrificial sibling in my younger years. He, too, has known my journey.

Other family members who have become dear to me after my mother's death and during the writing of this book are my cousin Brenda Wall and her mother, Aunt Louise Friesen. Brenda has become like a sister to me.

There are a host of friends whose shoulders I have stood upon at different times. The most constant has been my dear friend, Gayla Swingrover. We have been friends for 29 years and discovered we are also cousins. I've often wondered what the personification of love is truly like and my heart turns to find her friendship.

I have a broader band of friends that I will name, each bringing a wealth of love and support into my life. Dawn Angelich's spiritual insights have been a light since our meeting in 1973. Her calls and our visits are priceless; we are "kindred spirits." Pat Junge has been a godly example to me as a mother of six adult children and "adopted" mother for me. Debbie Driscoll, Jeanie Ganssle, Barb Borntrager, Debbie Horner, Dr. Katie Tuttle, Tarra Wellings, Debbie Osborn, Nancee Vermeer, Dee Maltby, Wendy Bush, Ruth Ann Graybill, Ana Lopez and Dawn Fielder are all women whom I admire and who have been part of my fabric of friendship, wisdom, and support. There are others who belong to this list as well.

I would be remiss if I did not thank my friends in my "travelling book club." Our only destination together to date has been Hawaii, where Dolores Godwin opened her home with hospitality and love. Although we have travelled to only one place, we have read many books. Our monthly meetings of friendship and literary critiques have been bundles of fun and joy. So to Nancy, Nancee, Lesa, Judi, Vivian, Dolores, and Sharon: Thanks for inviting me to join. I look forward to "hard-to-read and easy-to-read books" as well as places we may yet visit. I hope you read my book!

I also want to give a "shout out" to my Life Coach colleagues from the Del Mar, California 2008 Fast Track.

May God bless the many wonderful people I've met who share my struggles with anxiety and depression. I hope we connect through this writing.

God bless,
Beverlee Buller Keck

Preface

Overview

The title of this book, *Just One More Day: Meditations for Those Who Struggle with Anxiety and Depression*, grew out of a process of searching for the best way to encapsulate my story, the chapter entries, and the appendix of this book in just one phrase. Every person may take consolation in thinking about his or her life in terms of a "life message." If I were to identify my life message, it would be to live *Just One More Day*. That's why the first entry begins with this title. This choice to live just one more day has allowed me to persevere through times of intense darkness to see yet another glimmer of light that gives me hope to endure.

I recently asked a very prominent psychiatrist whether anxiety and depression were primarily situational or chemical; he answered, "Always both." There are other professionals with varying points of view. I believe there may be a propensity that is hardwired, and major triggers reveal the anxiety and depression that are already present, potentially inducing a "major depressive episode." While we can rarely control the triggers, we can learn to respond to them with better function.

I recently sat with friend who told me, "I do not want to be me." People who struggle with this kind of "mind pain" do not desire to be thus afflicted, no more than any sick person desires to be ill. Often the sufferer is left to him or herself with no resources to cope. I hope that this book provides both coping skills and encouragement.

I had never doubted my sense of meaning in light of the overall purposes of God until my major depressive episode began. I lost all sense of meaning as it relates to something bigger than I am. I came to believe that my contribution and life only took up space that could be better utilized by another. I've had to struggle at the deepest core with my sense of meaning. A brilliant professor of philosophy who teaches at Yale University explained to me that doubt and faith can co-exist, but the real enemy is *un*belief. I can't come up with a better argument for my existence than the Christian one. While I've had to accept the co-existing experience of both doubt and faith, I know that in spite of the battle, I believe.

Another fight that anxious and depressed folk battle is the seeming loss of potential. Parents look on and wonder why, in the prime of life, their son/daughter has to siphon off life and rearrange plans and hopes to bow to the complexities of these diseases. They mourn the loss of their children's potential. Adults who suffer with anxiety and depression mourn the loss of their own potential. In looking back on the road of anxiety and depression, we see the losses, not the gains, and our precious few years upon this planet seem devoted to these robbers. I have come to believe that my value is no less because I might do less. The world simply functions by a different standard than God's. Measuring our value by how well I do is not God's measuring stick. "Being" is as important to him as "doing." In the end, life is about who we become.

You will notice that in my book, I refer to "Covered Dishes." I first heard this reference made in the documentary *Shadow Voices: Finding Hope in Mental*

Illness. Dr. Joyce Burland, President of the National Alliance on Mental Illness, states, "Mental illness is the only disease where no one brings you a covered dish." How true of the invisible diseases of anxiety and depression. The pain of living can be greater than the pain of dying. I know—because I've been there. The "Covered Dish" idea refers to the image of food being delivered in covered baking dishes. There is nothing like food delivery to cheer a sick soul. The work of preparing a "covered dish" and bringing it to someone in need is one less burden for the patient to worry and care about.

The problem with anxiety and depression, however, is that they are invisible; we can't directly point to them. Because of this, a "covered dish" isn't always delivered.

In my book, I share the story of my battle with anxiety and depression. The daily meditations evolved as a result of my journey. Months into recovery, I began to realize that wellness will not involve the absence of anxiety; I will always experience a level of anxiety greater than the average person does. My goal is not to *eliminate* anxiety, but to *embrace* it, with its fluctuation and fluidity and for the unexpected strength that comes as a result.

The meditations have already proven to be life-giving. I mean this quite literally—one therapist, after using this material with a client, reported that it saved the client's life.

There is a growing awareness of the high incidence and debilitating effects of anxiety disorders. For example, Jane Chestnut, editor-in-chief of *Woman's Day*, recently "outed herself" as a sufferer of this type of disorder and resolved to feature special articles on this topic, treating issues of mental wellness as a new major cause the magazine now supports.

"Next time you're standing in the checkout line at the grocery store or stuck in traffic, take a look around. Chances are, the person behind you knows—or is—someone who has had depression or anxiety. Nearly 19% of American adults struggle with an anxiety disorder and 5 to 8% deal with depression in a given year. Women are at least two times as likely as men to experience these conditions." —Woman's Day, *May 6, 2008*

With numbers running this high, there are two kinds of readers: those who suffer and those who know people who do. Those who know people who suffer include professional and lay counsellors, as well as family and friends.

What Readers Will Gain

The Reader will experience personal validation.
Readers will realize they do not suffer in anxiety and
depression alone. Readers will experience true empathy
in their "awful feelings." Readers will identify with
the thoughts, feelings, and experiences I've expressed
throughout the book.

The Reader will experience moments of relief. Through
the Scripture readings, meditations, action steps, and
prayers, readers will be able to recognize and confront
distorted thought patterns and feelings and engage in
activities to help reduce them and provide some relief.

The Reader will experience hope. Readers can draw
upon untapped resources to survive depression and
anxiety by allowing a refreshing new kind of creativity
to emerge. Each meditation helps motivate readers
to look up in expectant hope instead of down in
frustration and despair.

My Story

This is my story of what it has been like to suffer catastrophic anxiety and a major depressive episode. It's my anguish and it is certainly not meant to be prescriptive or prophetic. I'm no one special; I am just a typical person. But I seek to reach out to those who are suffering by sharing my own journey through the valleys of depression and anxiety. I'm convinced that I'm not alone; in fact, I'm *sure* I'm not alone.

I had been struggling desperately because of the potential threat of losing my job. The ramifications bled into all the worst scenarios of financial collapse. In the face of this reality, my focus and deepest insecurities were realized. I had a genetic predisposition to anxiety and depression; it began to intensify as a result of extensive work travel and isolation from family and friends. The anxiety was unmanageable; in fact, it had become debilitating.

Despite experiencing periods when I functioned well, I also experienced periods of severe dysfunction. This fluctuation in my ability to function was so disturbing that I began to experience periods of physical desperation caused by loss of sleep and appetite. Rising early in the morning was leaving me exhausted during the day and my concentration was minimal. I confided in no one about how bad things really were. It seemed too risky to tell anyone for fear I would lose my job. In January 2007, my boss informed me that the business had to evaluate its financial bottom line. As a result, my fear of losing my job intensified. I kept this information to myself, and I did not know where to turn for help.

The death of my mother followed in February that year, which was layered with deep feelings of loss and disorientation. This added to the already shaky ground upon which my mind stood. The adjustment of returning to my job responsibilities seemed empty compared to the slow death my mother suffered. She died after a 14-year battle with Parkinson's disease. Her departure was not peaceful. She barely uttered words and fought death; the nursing staff thought her heart had stopped several times when, in fact, it was still beating. The six days I sat by her side were incubation from the fears of my job, but extremely visually disturbing. My mother's body was skin on bones because of her inability to eat in her condition.

My internal compass of life was no longer pointing north. My emotions began to slide, and by March, I was beginning to report intense periods of anxiety without relief. I confided in several therapists and the subject of a medical leave became a topic of conversation that I wanted to avoid. My job hung in the balance already; how would a medical leave eventually affect the outcome? The following describes how my experience played out by August of that year.

I was terrified. I couldn't get back on track. I felt as if my mind was an ice skater that fell and couldn't get up. The physical sensation I experienced was sheer panic. It felt as if someone was shooting poison into my veins; it was such a visceral experience and a sensation of mortal terror. The crawling sense of panic was heightening. Physical and mental pain tore through me. I was frightened by the real and the unreal; my mind had split over trying to determine the difference.

My husband and I drove through traffic to my
therapist's appointment. I finally decided to tell the
therapist how bad I was feeling; I couldn't stand it
anymore. The words of desperation rolled rapidly off
my tongue. Whatever I said, it was the right choice.
Within several days and after seeing several therapists, a
psychiatrist issued an immediate medical leave from my
company. By the week's end, the appropriate documents
had been signed by my company. I hated this and I
could not see my way through, so I slumped into bed to
escape the reality of what was happening to me.

I felt empty and alone, experiencing anxiety, always
anxiety. I moved through the day sort of dancing with
anxiety. I would momentarily leave the dance and focus
on something else, and then return to the dance. It
was like losing my place in line all the time and then
returning and going to the back of the line; I never
reached the front. This dance represented a metaphor
for distraction from life and reality. I needed healing—
major healing.

For more than a year, I had carried the same file,
containing a year's worth of pertinent documentation
that represented the ragged edges of my life. It
held medical records, documents that I copied,
diagrams drawn by my therapist, a general reference
to antidepressants and their selective action on
neurotransmitters, and the transcripts of a broadcast
aired on "Family Life Today" featuring Pastor Tommy
Nelson (the first broadcast, entitled "Falling Into
Darkness," aired three days after I was placed on
medical leave, August 27, 2007).

Miraculously, during the fluctuation of this time, I wrote "sanity savers" via entries in my journal. The principles were the muscles I used to keep me moving. The first entry is my "Popeye" muscle: "Just Live One More Day." These entries became the book you are about to read. Not all are about aching despair; I tried to write about things I knew would be helpful to those suffering from anxiety and depression. I did not want to focus exclusively on my depressive episode.

My feelings about my writing are sacred and frayed. Each entry brings a memory of a gagging sense of compromised mental and physical capacity. Although I made progress in the healing process, it was at a snail's pace.

My medical leave created immediate relief; however, my sense of relief was short-lived. It was an immediate and temporary solution because the feeling of relief soon dissipated. God seemed to be speaking to me in themes, criss-crossing information that was in agreement. A week into my leave, a friend heard of my situation and paid for me to attend a Women of Faith pre-conference, entitled "God Has a Dream for Your Life." I humbly accepted the invitation. I had never previously attended this conference.

Somewhat skeptical, I attended. How did my fall into an emotional abyss have anything to do with this pre-conference? But as I sat in the Honda Center, I felt transported, as if airlifted out of a terrible car accident to the safety of a hospital. A week prior, I had been fully focused on my fall business travel schedule and job responsibilities. But all of that faded away as I sat in the conference in a state of shock, transfixed.

I felt safe and incubated sitting between two friends. I had no emotional skin on. I wanted to hide and listen at the same time. Sheila Walsh spoke of confronting the pain of her childhood and Dr. Henry Cloud spoke about the recovery of personal dreams. I had no dreams, only nightmares. Deep in my soul, I knew God was talking to me. I was miles from the Promised Land, but God had a plan for me, starting with hearing the profound testimonies of hope and recovery from anxiety and depression.

After the conference, I knew I needed to face my anxiety and depression head on, but wasn't sure how to go about it. No rulebook existed to guide me through a medical leave. All I had to work with was the doctor's recommendations. This left me with a lot of unstructured time to dwell in my despair.

Counselling was one of the recommendations. I brought confused assumptions, fears, irrational certainties, and self-deprecation into my therapy, and they all grew in intensity as the week progressed. In therapy, I discovered how disjointed my thinking had become. My therapist specialized in cognitive therapy, something with which I was not even familiar. Little did I know it would be the answer to some of my distorted thinking.

In an effort to stabilize me emotionally, my doctor also recommended antidepressants, exercise, and rest. I wrestled with various antidepressants; some made me feel dizzy or nauseated. I struggled to find a suitable medication that did not cause undesirable side-effects. I also started water aerobics at the local YMCA, joining the senior group, which was at a pace I could maintain, as I had not exercised in years.

Sometimes, just *existing* was my only success (I would call these "DVD days"—but I rationalized that sitting and watching movies is better than self-inflicted pain). I would ask a friend to come sit with me so I was not alone.

One pivotal event occurred weeks into my leave when I contracted a nasty case of the flu. It was as if I had contracted a deadly virus; I had no fight left. My meagre efforts to provide meals for my family fell off the table; I had resorted to fast food. I put away all inhibition and pride and called a bygone friend who seemed safe and asked for a cooked meal. I called the right person; for the next two months, suppers arrived in beautiful presentation. I would try to pick up the house and wait for her face and our meal, my "Covered Dishes." As much as I appreciated the meals, I appreciated the renewed friendship that developed even more.

During my leave, I constantly worried about our financial well-being. What impact would all this have on my job security? There was no simple solution. I obsessed over the threat of financial ruin. I had moved from medical leave to short-term disability. How does a practitioner determine wellness when it is not visible to the naked eye? My genetics and biochemistry had locked arms and created catastrophic anxiety. It was like being hit over the head with a sledgehammer to learn that I would not be aspiring to a state of calmness. At best, my anxiety and depression would be above normal; I would always have anxiety and experience it on some level. Moving forward, my "new normal," did not mean the absence of anxiety; it meant learning to function, *despite* anxiety. This diagnosis was both a relief and noose because it was a reality and it was something I could understand, but it was also something that would not entirely go away.

Hey, God? Did you have something to do with my hardwiring? I would venture to the Almighty. *Hey, God? Did you have something to do with my birth chain? Hey, God? Is this your idea of weaving me in my mother's womb* (Psalm 139:13)*? Couldn't there have been a better yarn selection?*

In retrospect, God used everything and everyone to help me during my journey of anxiety and depression. Etched in my mind is the day my "Covered Dish" friend mentioned the name Randy Pausch to me as we crossed the street on a hot summer day. I was inspired by his book, *Last Lecture.* Randy's words seemed to connect with this slippery theme of dreaming dreams, and even though I continued having nightmares, God's quiet voice seemed to speak to me about dreams and hopes. I loved this quote from Randy Pausch: "The brick walls are not there to keep us out; the brick walls are there to give us a chance to show how badly we want something. The brick walls are there to stop the people who don't want it badly enough."

What a contrary way of thinking; obstacles are a *filter.* This made sense to me, and it seemed consistent with biblical thought, too. Jesus often asked people who were sick if they wanted to be healed. This was a no-brainer, but the real question was *how much* they wanted healing (Mark 10:49-52). I languished over the thoughts of not getting well.

I have a journal in which I documented my daily anxiety level based on a scale of one to 10, with one being calm and 10 being extremely anxious. I kept these records for almost nine months. Shortly into my leave, a therapist friend told me "a major depressive episode" lasts six months to a year. I gasped in shock at the time, but time has proved it surprisingly true. My therapist told me I would experience anything and everything three times as severely as the average person would. I made some false starts. I had the opportunity to enter long-term disability, but my therapist informed me that patients who do that begin to define themselves as "disabled." I passed on this option at the time and decided to fight. Fight for my life, fight for a job, fight for my family!

It made sense that the tides of my anxiety would ebb by day's end and flow in the morning. I had to consciously confront my anxious thoughts each and every day. The stairs leading to my office became like the "green mile." I cringed at the very sight of my desk. This office was the most beautiful self-standing structure when I first saw it. But now it represented terror, the terror that started there and the anxiety that had begun to wallop my brain. The adrenalin flowed through my body for days without a break, as though terrorists were threatening my very being.

My dear friend kept warning me that I was doing too much. Despite his apprehension, my husband periodically talked to me about taking a leave of absence from my job, but I kept on going out of sheer determination and fear of losing my job. There were times I functioned very well. Conversely, there were times the anxiety would render me out of commission. I felt such self-induced pressure to conceal my depression and anxiety and appear "normal." However, I was so lonely and felt total desperation.

What became most profound during this time was the network of friends that came to my aid. They were, and continue to be, a strong and secure bucket under my own leaking bucket. My therapist told me that people with anxiety feel as though their bucket has five holes in the bottom through which everything runs. Nothing truer has been said to me. These women have held my water. Put them all in one room and we could solve the world's problems with their wisdom. These are my heroines, all for different reasons.

I understand how someone moves toward social phobia because I have experienced it. It's too risky to relate to others when you have no emotional defences. I felt as though I would fall to my knees with the slightest mess-up or sideways glance. I wanted to become a recluse for the rest of my life. I needed no notoriety, nor did I desire any. I wanted absolute seclusion, which is strange for a person who normally derives all her energy from people.

I would never suggest that I'm not vulnerable to relapse. But through God's grace, the help of doctors and therapists, and the unconditional love and support of family and cherished friends, I have been able to find my way to the road of recovery. It is my heart's desire to share with you the principles that have helped me on my journey through depression and anxiety. May God bless you and keep you!

Wait One More Day

Scripture

"I would have despaired unless I had believed that I would see the goodness of the Lord, in the land of the living. Wait for the Lord; be strong and let your heart take courage; yes, wait for the Lord." PSALM 27:13-14 (NASB)

"I would rather be strangled – rather die than suffer like this. But, when it is uprooted, it's as though it never existed! That's the end of its life, and others spring up from the earth to replace it. But look, God will not reject a person of integrity, nor will He lend a hand to the wicked. He will once again fill your mouth with laughter and your lips with shouts of joy. Those who hate you will be clothed with shame, and the home of the wicked will be destroyed."
JOB 7:15, 8:18-22 (NLT)

"As He passed by, He saw a man blind from birth. And His disciples asked Him, 'Rabbi, who sinned, this man or his parents, that he would be born blind?' Jesus answered, 'It was neither that this man sinned, nor his parents; but it was so that the works of God might be displayed in him. We must work the works of Him who sent me as long as it is day; night is coming when no one can work.'"
JOHN 9:1-4 (NASB)

Meditation

My therapist was late because he was intently involved in a conversation with a colleague about a patient who was threatening suicide. I listened as they talked. My therapist said that while a person usually ruminates on the *idea* and *thoughts* of suicide, the act itself is generally impulsive. He also said that a person may not take his or her life while in a "deep valley," but rather during a frightening relapse of depression after experiencing some recovery. Suicide is not a cop-out in the mind of the sufferer; it is a perceived solution to a problem he or she can't solve.

Suicide has touched my life in a profound way. A fellow participant in a small study group took his life. My dear friend lost his son to suicide. I recently heard about another loss of life due to suicide. Even Christian leaders take their lives.

I know the night can be black when we are depressed. But what is making us feel this despair? Why do we feel so utterly hopeless? Even answering such questions may frighten us. We may feel there is something we *should* do, but *can't*. The inaction itself is enough to overwhelm our psyches. Then, the "shoulds" set in. We *should* be this, we *should* be like that, we *should* not do that, we *should* have done that. Thoughts about ourselves become distorted: We forget who we are and all the joys in our lives and instead focus on, and become overwhelmed with, all our mistakes and failures. We experience "mind pain," which is self-recrimination and self-loathing. "If only someone knew how horrible I feel about myself," we think.

Viktor E. Frankl writes in *Man's Search for Meaning*, "As a young doctor, I spent four years in Austria's largest state hospital, where I was in charge of the pavilion in which severely depressed patients were accommodated—most of them having been admitted after a suicide attempt. I once calculated that I must have explored 12,000 patients during those four years. Whenever I am confronted with someone who is prone to suicide, I explain to such a person that patients have repeatedly told me how happy they were that the suicide attempt had not been successful; weeks, months, years later, they told me, it turned out that there was a solution to their problem, an answer to their question, a meaning to their life" (Viktor E. Frankl, *Man's Search for Meaning*, Beacon Press, Boston, 1959, p. 142). Frankl goes on to assure the patient that he or she may be the one to live to see the day dawn in which he or she finds his or her answer.

There is a song written by Wilson Phillips, entitled "Hold On." The lyrics say, "Can you hold on for one more day, things'll go your way, hold on for one more day" (Glen Ballard, Wilson Philips, *Hold On*, SBK Records, 1990). The Psalmist gives a shout out in Psalm 27: "Wait for the Lord." If our depression is so bad that all we can do is just *Wait One More Day*, then that is success with a capital "S."

I remember the first time Psalm 27 bore a hole into my soul. I was sitting on a rock, watching lizards scurry about. This Psalm leapt into my lap just as fast as a lizard would have. I say to you, my depressed friends, just wait another day. I have experienced the results of waiting one more day. If we choose to wait just one more day, we might find a delicious meal under the covered dish of life we never thought we would taste. We are worth the wait. We are worth what we need.

Action Step

Hang on to God. Just wait one more day, even if you think you can't.

Prayer

Lord, help me to live another day, hour by hour, even moment by moment. If I can choose another hour, I can choose another day. Even though I feel despair, I may feel less despair tomorrow. You are the God who made me and can provide meaning for my life. Help me to hold on because of You.

My Journal

My Journal

Cling On

Scripture

"For You have been my help, and in the shadow of Your wings I sing for joy. My soul clings to You; Your right hand upholds me." PSALM 63:7-8 (NASB)

"I will not leave you as orphans; I will come to you." JOHN 14:18 (NASB)

Meditation

Anorexia nervosa and bulimia are prevalent in our culture. Those afflicted may not trust their decisions or value themselves and tend to view the world in a black-and-white state, like TV before colour. They deeply need to please others. They may even sabotage their success because they are afraid they can't maintain the skills they need to sustain it.

I was sitting in a support group meeting for friends and families of those with eating disorders. The chatter was bouncing around the room like a tossed ball. I nestled in the corner of the couch and listened to the smart hearts that shared. The good doctor leading the group had just the right pinch of this-and-that to make for a recipe of good-tasting food for thought among those who do not eat.

One young woman began to discuss her journey and said that in relationships, she left "claw marks"—I visualized a cat sliding down a wall, never getting a grip to stop. Fear of rejection and abandonment reign in the minds of those with eating disorders. I understand this dependency need. Sometimes I feel like a "cling on" (those little fabric dryer sheets) in relationships because my feeling of need is so profound. I'm afraid to say how much I need because it may be too great for anyone to fill. I appear quite content, all the while wanting to cling, wanting someone to fill that hole. But who can satiate this need?

This need is so intense because we fear abandonment; we fear having to stand alone. It is a basic human need to want connection, belonging, and attachment. There is nothing wrong with it; we were never meant to be alone. In fact, the God of the universe, who walked the Garden of Eden with Adam, said it was not good for Adam to be alone. We would think that God provided everything Adam needed. But at the end of the day, after naming all of the animals, God knew Adam would hang his head and say, "Who do I relate to here?"

Some of us feel the "hole in the soul" more deeply than others do, creating anxiety and depression. There are times when we do have to be alone, but we can always cling to God. In Psalms, David said he clung to the Lord. The Lord is not needy or co-dependent; he is only a giver. The word "cling" in Psalm 63 literally means "to cleave, adhere, to be glued." We can super-glue ourselves to God. We can cling on like "fabric cling" right out of the dryer, and he will not shake us off.

Only God can fill the hole in our souls. Jesus promised He would come to us and dwell in us so we would never be alone.

Action Step

Find a way to deliberately be alone with God. Draw a picture of yourself stuck to God. Art can provide small relief in the midst of anxiety or depression.

Prayer

Lord, I am so glad that I can cling to You and You never tire of my need. No one else can save me. No one else can fill the hole in my soul. You are inexhaustible when others have limited resources. Lord, I cling to You.

My Journal

Self-Care

Scripture

"As the deer pants for the waterbrooks, so my soul pants for You, O God." PSALM 42:1 (NASB)

Meditation

I read the book *Down Came the Rain* by supermodel/actress Brooke Shields. I'm far beyond postpartum depression, but the onset of depression that gripped Brooke after the birth of her baby caused me to think. Inside the cover of her book, I listed all of the changes, transitions, and crises I have experienced in the last three years, and was appalled.

There is a prescription for those who suffer from Post-Traumatic Stress Disorder (PTSD). It is a reminder to stay safe in our minds, safe in our bodies, and safe in our environment. When we truly do not know what to do, we can return to self-care. Imagine yourself as a deer in search of water—this is much like the need for self-care. Self-care feels so contrary to pushing ahead. We might think self-care is like eating bowls of ice cream when there is so much work to be done. No, we have to drink water before we can continue our journey over the hills and valleys of life.

A friend once told me, "Treat yourself as a separate soul. Treat yourself like you would treat a friend who is suffering with this." It's true—we are generally so much nicer to others than we are to ourselves. We continue to demand from our bodies what they are incapable of producing at times.

Self-care is difficult to implement because it is so counterintuitive. Our first instinct is to do more, push harder, and "keep on keeping-on." We fear losing our sense of competence or worry about the frustration of non-productivity. However, refuelling is the key to productivity.

I knew I was tired one day—the kind of bone-weary tired that goes from head to toe. I got out of bed and asked myself what I needed. My most urgent need was to see a friend and get away for a drive before making some important phone calls and sending some emails. I knew I needed to write. I knew I needed some energy tea. I chose to put the phone calls and emails on hold and self-soothe.

Action Step

Pick one of the following: Take a walk around a block or in a park and let your eyes rest on something pretty. Say the kindest thing you can think of to yourself. Call someone you love and chat. Browse around a bookstore. Go to a movie or rent one and watch it. Stay safe today in body, mind, and soul.

Prayer

Lord, I feel so guilty about taking care of myself; guilt, always guilt. Help me to assign the worth You assign to me. Help me to have victory over guilt so that I can take care of my needs. Help me to believe I am worth what I need and live it.

My Journal

The Future

Scripture

"For I know the plans that I have for you," declares the Lord, "plans for welfare and not for calamity to give you a future and a hope. Then you will call upon Me and come and pray to Me, and I will listen to you." JEREMIAH 29:11-12 (NASB)

"If I should say, 'My foot has slipped,' Your lovingkindness, O Lord, will hold me up. When my anxious thoughts multiply within me, Your consolations delight my soul." PSALM 94:18 -19 (NASB)

Meditation

I know better than to take verses, such as Jeremiah 29:11, out of context. I was a seminary student in a hermeneutics (the study of biblical interpretation) class once upon a time. By the time the semester was over, all of my well-worn Scriptures had taken on new meaning because I learned to study the verses in the context of the passage. Jeremiah 29:11 is a worn-out verse. I think some "well-worn" verses demonstrate the very essence of God's nature. Note in verse 10 of this passage that God's promise will come in 70 years!

The meaning is still, like clear-blue sky. God is about life and a *real*—not a fake—tomorrow. He wants a meaningful tomorrow for his people: then, now, and for us. He is the God of restoration. God has stated that he can make up for the years the locusts have eaten, when they have eaten up the very health of our lives.

Depressed people have trouble visualizing the future. We have difficulty imagining a better tomorrow. When troubles arise, we tend to "catastrophize" and "futurize;" there is no "I'll cross that bridge when I get there." We're standing on the bridge while it's swaying, the water below is rising, the rain is falling, and we're not sure if this crossing will be our last. The "what ifs" get louder and louder, even shouting, in our heads.

Psalm 94:19 is of great consolation here. What if our feet slip on the bridge? The Lord's loving kindness will hold us up. What if "Old Faithful"—anxiety—starts to blow, getting the better of us? God will console us, helping to confront the distortions of our thoughts.

I have realized that at any life stage, God has a hopeful future for me. It rattled my cage at first when I became a "senior." *How does God have a future for me when two thirds of my life is spent?* I wondered. *I go to a restaurant and now I'm eligible for reduced fares between 4:00pm and 6:00pm because I'm a senior? This is absurd!* The whole empty-nest thing is a hard pill to swallow, too. Further, my mother's death put me at the top of the ladder with no one above me. I'm slowly trying to climb down, but I felt like I was hitting a brick wall. *What's left for me on this planet? What do I have to offer? Do I matter?*

The future does not have to be about our exit. It can involve painting a colourful stroke of hopes and dreams. It can involve creating a list of the things that would make us happy. Maybe some of those wishes are on a shelf out of reach; maybe others are at arm's length. But reaching for those desires creates a better chance of bringing some of our hopes and dreams down to our level. If we don't try, things will never change for the better. It is worth the effort; *we* are worth the effort!

Action Step

Make a list of the things that would make you happy and try to achieve one of them. One therapist asks his clients to make a list of 50 "I wants." Take some time today and create that list of 50 "I wants."

Prayer

Lord, help me to value the things that bring me happiness. Help me to choose to work toward a goal I want to accomplish. Help me to have the strength to share my desires and to act to achieve them. Help me to remember that You take joy in my happiness.

My Journal

Image Bearers

Scripture

"My frame was not hidden from You, when I was made in secret, and skillfully wrought in the depths of the earth; Your eyes have seen my unformed substance; and in Your book they were all written, the days that were ordained for me, when as yet there was not one of them." PSALM 139:15-16 (NASB)

"You were knitted together. You aren't an accident. You weren't mass-produced. You aren't an assembly line product." MAX LUCADO

Meditation

The greatest journey we will embark on is the discovery of our sense of "self." Self is what becomes buried in the sludge of life. My life has been a difficult journey, and I wonder if I am leaving a clear template of myself for my daughter.

Self-doubt may constantly plague us. Our sense of "self" is like a kite we hang on to but that seems to want to get away. We have to hang on tight at times, lest it take off without us in the whipping, fast-changing winds.

In the movie *The Runaway Bride*, potential bride Maggie (Julia Roberts) kept avoiding the altar. She had been the hippie bride-to-be, the conservative bride-to-be, and the sports enthusiast bride-to-be. But Ike (Richard Gere), the reporter from New York, blew her cover, accusing her of not having her own mind and, in particular, not knowing what type of eggs she liked, as she had always picked her fiancés' favourites. Maggie began to discover herself by determining her egg preference. She tried all the possibilities and ultimately decided she preferred eggs benedict. In the end, Maggie turned over her running shoes to the man who "got" her and married Ike.

Much like the runaway bride, we often don't know who we are or what we want and we are afraid to stay true to ourselves.

We may feel like chameleons who adapt to mirror those around us, changing our "self" as appropriate. However, we need to learn to know what *we* think—not everyone else. One of the greatest losses caused by anxiety is the loss of "self". We can hear everyone's input except our own. Once the adrenalin kicks in, our minds shut off. The anxiety is crawling and we let it guide us. It's so painful that we give in to the anxiety, even if it means disagreeing with our own thoughts, feelings, and opinions.

Reflecting on my young adulthood, I have concluded that my anxiety left me vulnerable. But I want wellness, and that may mean a choice that displeases others. I imagine that in heaven, I will have the full "me" of my "I." It's not always God whom I long for, but my sense of self that seems to be lost. It takes amazing guts to *really* live life; to live without a self, without an identity, is next to impossible.

I truly believe that fear is what stands between us and knowing who we are. We are afraid of what might happen, of what we might feel, in discovering our true selves. We want to run from anxiety and the discomfort that "self search" involves. However, tolerating uncomfortable feelings can be a part of the self-discovery process.

One woman in an eating disorder support group shared that when she was first hospitalized, she had to eat a meal and then sit with the feeling of being full. She said it felt as if she had a bowl of worms in her stomach. We may feel as if we have a "bowl of worms in our stomachs" during this self-discovery process, which will probably make us want to run from the uncomfortable feelings. But we must sit with our feelings and buy time.

Buying time is not meant as an escape hatch. But sometimes we are able to find ourselves when we rely on our God-given ability to rationalize. We can think things through and come to trust our own voice. Our voice does not have to sound like the voices of those around us. We have our *own* thoughts, wishes, and desires. We may feel like a "deer in the headlights" about our thinking. If so, a remedial step may be to write what we think, with the goal of eventually being able to speak what we think. An authentic self, rather than a false self, is a much better representation of the image of God. An authentic self is one God works on as He dismantles our addictions and dependencies over time. A false self is what we erect to fabricate something of personal meaning. We may choose that through our career or any other agent that provides meaning. It is like building walls and a roof with no foundation. There is a point and a process: The point is when we realize we have made a misery of things and the process is God's repair and restoration of who we are in Him.

Depression masks the real us. But we need to remove that layer, like wiping the mud off a painting to see what the artist had in mind. We want to be able to say with the daughter in the book *Fingernail Moon*, "I love my *Self*" and "I love you, God" (*Fingernail Moon*, Janie Webster, Shaw Books, 1998).

Action Step

Write down something you know to be true about yourself and share this truth with someone you trust.

Prayer

Lord, sometimes my anxiety is so exhausting, I can't hear myself think. Only You can relieve me from this torment. I ask You, Lord, to please do so. I'm easily swayed and tend to think what others think, do what they do, and say what they say. Give me the courage and strength to say what I want to say and do what I need to do. Only You can relieve me from this torment. I ask You, Lord, to please do so.

My Journal

My Journal

Wit's End: Community

Scripture

"He led them also by a straight way, to go to an inhabited city. They reeled and staggered like a drunken man, and were at their wit's end. Then they cried to the Lord in their trouble, and He brought them out of their distresses. So he guided them to their desired haven." PSALM 107:7A, 27-28, 30B (NASB)

"No temptation has overtaken you but such as is common to man; and God is faithful, who will not allow you to be tempted beyond what you are able, but with the temptation will provide the way of escape also, so that you will be able to endure it." I COR. 10:13 (NASB)

Meditation

This is a most beautiful chapter (Psalm 107). I would encourage you to read the entire Psalm before you consider this meditation. Notice that God led the Israelites to an inhabited city, not a desolate ghost town where everyone had disappeared. This entire Psalm sums up God's relationship with the rebellious Israelites. But note that the deepest need was a place of belongingness—"a desired haven."

I read a chapter in the book *Life Without Ed: How One Woman Declared Independence from Her Eating Disorder and How You Can Too*. Jenni Schaefer, the author, says, "There is no such thing as too much support and none of us can do it alone." I agree. I believe in sponsors, support groups, community, togetherness—there is strength in numbers.

Isolation has been a difficult issue for me. I did not realize what was happening as it was happening. Our family moved, which relocated us geographically. We left a school program in which my daughter was involved for years. In addition, I was a "remote employee" for my company, having little or no contact with others. My feelings of isolation deepened when my mother died, and my family of origin went through deep loss on many levels.

Henri Nouwen, who authored *The Inner Voice of Love*, my favourite among many other of his gems, moved to L'Arche (an intentional community for the mentally disabled) at the age of 50. He had been a Harvard professor and a spiritual director his entire life, and went through his greatest period of anguish after age 50! He catalogues this in *The Inner Voice*. I'm discovering and building community little by little, just as Nouwen chose by his move.

Our communities are not organic; we are transplants. We find ourselves in church on Sundays coming from every direction. Normally, we have no reason to cross paths during our week; therefore, creating community must become a very intentional issue. I asked a friend to describe her organic community; she named a few people and was startled by her sense of isolation. This is not God's design. Another friend of mine, a university professor, had a Nigerian student in her class who tried to translate the word "isolation" to his family upon a visit home. He could find no equivalent word for it in his language. His village could not understand the concept of isolation.

God did not design for us to live in isolation but to be in *community*. Community teaches us that we are all, in some way or another, going through the same thing, and that we can go through the trials and tribulations of life together. The enemy of our souls, however, wants us to hide our suffering, and we persist in the lie that we are alone in our dilemmas.

We are pulled deeper toward isolation by the gravitational forces of anxiety and depression. But the benefits of engagement far outweigh isolation. Maybe at "wit's end," we will finally risk reaching out unashamedly.

precipitators (triggers) → provoke anxiety and depression
precipitators + isolation → depression
precipitators + human connection → joy

Action Step

First, identify someone you know who may be isolated and reach out to him or her. Second, describe a benefit of engagement. Take note of something encouraging that came from conversation or a shared activity. Try to strengthen the "muscle" of engagement.

Prayer

Lord, I want to run from the depression and hide away. I feel conflicted about being with others, but I know it is not good for me to be alone in life. Help me to choose friends and family who can comfort me and who are willing to listen when I need their help.

My Journal

_____

_____

_____

_____

_____

_____

_____

_____

_____

_____

_____

_____

_____

_____

_____

_____

_____

_____

_____

Back-Up Plans for Provision

Scripture

"Thus the Lord saved Israel that day from the hand of the Egyptians, and Israel saw the Egyptians dead on the seashore. When Israel saw the great power which the Lord had used against the Egyptians, the people feared the Lord, and they believed in the Lord and in His servant Moses."
EXODUS 14:30-31 (NASB)

"Not that I speak from want, for I have learned to be content in whatever circumstances I am in." PHILIPPIANS 4:11. (NASB)

"I have been young and now I am old, yet I have not seen the righteous forsaken, or his descendants begging for bread."
PSALM 37:25 (NASB)

"Look at the birds of the air that they do not sow, nor reap, nor gather into barns and yet your heavenly Father feeds them. Are you not worth much more than they?"
MATTHEW 6:26 (NASB)

Meditation

I've thought about the Israelites, standing at the shore of the Red Sea, the Egyptians behind them, and no back-up plan. The Egyptians weren't just galloping their horses; they were *whipping* them at top speed. Visualize an animal that has been taunted and then finally lunges at his prey. This was the state of the Egyptian army. "Let my people go," had been riveted into the Pharaoh's psyche through the threat of frogs and blood. Pharaoh was hot on the Israelites' trail. Can't you just picture an Israelite looking down at his feet in the water with the sound of chariots behind him? Back-up plan?! No, he was standing in wet sandals with sweat pouring down his face and his heart throbbing, saying his last rites.

Maslow's hierarchy of needs places the basics of survival (food, water, shelter) as the most foundational layer of life. I have always been very vulnerable to my survival needs being threatened because at one point, they were. I was, figuratively speaking, left at the train station. There was nothing there when I was the neediest. A threat of job loss or a stab at our financial stability, and I'm on my knees. I do not take provision in stride.

This past year, I learned the hard way why job loss is rated up there with death and divorce. I lost money in the 2008/09 stock market debacle, as did many other North Americans. I read a very sad article in the newspaper conveying the desperation of an entrepreneur who shot himself and his family as a result of losing a large sum of money during the stock market fall.

My own grandfather attempted to take his life during the Great Depression. My mother and aunt were in charge of keeping him from harming himself. He lost everything and was unable to provide for his family. A friend's uncle lost his job during the Great Depression at the age of 59; he chose to sit in a rocking chair and never left it. His gainfully employed adult daughter lived at home and took care of him and his wife.

My friend told me of a time when she and her husband lost hundreds of thousands of dollars in investments while living the high life in a penthouse. As a result, they relocated to a small city, gave up a money-centred life in exchange for cutting coupons, and learned to split ample portions while dining out. "It was then we entered into a life of abundance," she said.

There are times when our only back-up plan is God. There are too many tight places in life for us to cover all of our bases. We overly responsible types try to cover God's bases, too, but we need to remember that there are things only *we* can do and there are things only *he* can do. Read Exodus 14—the only thing Moses did was stretch out his hand and God did all the rest.

Action Step

Meditate on Exodus 14 and 15. Determine what it is that only God can do and what it is that only you can do regarding provision. Sometimes during financial loss, we discover what truly matters and we reprioritize.

Our need for community appropriately intensifies our definition as abundance changes.

I have kept a "gratefulness journal" during this period of emotional deprivation. I am amazed by, and thankful for, the blessings God has bestowed upon me and the wonderful relationships I have in my life; they are priceless. You might want to begin a gratefulness journal, too.

Prayer

Lord, You performed miracles for countless people in the Bible, and I know You can perform miracles in my life. Help me to share my needs as well as trust. God, provide the financial resources I need to live. Help me to be grateful for what I have and to expect new provision, Lord, as You told your disciples to pray for "daily bread."

My Journal

My Journal

Meet Addie

Scripture

"Be anxious for nothing, but in everything by prayer and supplication with thanksgiving let your requests be made known to God. And the peace of God, which surpasses all comprehension, will guard your hearts and your minds in Christ Jesus. Finally, brethren, whatever is true, whatever is honorable, whatever is right, whatever is pure, whatever is lovely, whatever is of good repute, if there is any excellence and if anything worthy of praise, dwell on these things." PHILIPPIANS 4:6-8 (NASB)

"Therefore there is now no condemnation for those who are in Christ Jesus." ROMANS 8:1 (NASB)

Meditation

I want to introduce you to somebody named Addie. Addie is invisible, but wow, what a voice! Addie isn't very nice to me. In fact, she can be downright mean. Addie doesn't have enough to do with her own time, so she constantly tries to occupy mine. Addie feeds off the negative and creates all kinds of terrifying scenarios in my head that make me anxious. If I have an opinion, hers is generally just the opposite. If I've made a decision, she constantly questions my judgment. Addie hates to be alone in her misery, so she beckons to me to join her.

Addie can be the voice of depression. She likes to say whatever she wants, whenever she wants, and she is not respectful of my "head space" or my sanity. Addie loves to condemn me and tell me that I don't know what I think—that my ideas are simply inferior compared to everyone else's. She tells me I don't deserve things. Addie can literally stop me dead in my tracks. Addie also likes to remind me of my mistakes. Addie has a memory like a steel grate. She has no mercy. Nothing ever gets past her. She is right there to tie my head into a knot.

Addie has taken away my confidence and courage at the most inopportune moments. It is the will of Addie that I live in constant fear. Addie is the culmination of negative thinking.

I've lived with Addie for a very long time. Addie does remind me of people I know. She can sound "like the voice in my head" that was a frightened mother or other voices of critics. The way I ascribed such a distinct personality to her came from reading *Life Without Ed*. This book is a profound and humorous true tale of an individual who begins to give a unique personality to her eating disorder. I began to distinguish in myself a constant barrage of second-guessing and was shocked at how much this habit occupied my mind. I decided to distinguish between Addie's voice and that of my own objective self.

The technique of ignoring her voice and listening to truth, confronting my thoughts and considering their source, is a daily effort. I'm finding more "head space" because I'm not entertaining her very anxious manipulations. My goal is that these negatives occupy a small room and not my entire house.

Action Step

It may be helpful to experiment with personifying the distinct messages that you tell yourself. These negative messages are not consistent with truth. You have value because you are valuable—God created you with intrinsic worth. Choose the recovery of thought and begin renewing your mind. Choose to interrupt the patterns of negative thinking with thoughts of truth. Begin to realize that anxiety and depression is not *all* of who you are, even though it can feel that way. Identify that God has given you talents, gifts, and a personality *apart* from anxiety.

Prayer

Lord, today I make my requests known to You, even though I know You know my needs. Each day brings different pressures and challenges. It is hard not to dwell on the negatives and think good thoughts. Help me to dwell on what is true—not what is false. Help me to wait for Your peace.

My Journal

Anger

Scripture

"Then the earth shook and quaked; and the foundations of the mountains were trembling and were shaken, because He was angry." PSALM 18:7 (NASB)

"This you know, my beloved brethren. But everyone must be quick to hear, slow to speak and slow to anger; for the anger of man does not achieve the righteousness of God." JAMES 1:19-20 (NASB)

"Be angry, and yet do not sin; do not let the sun go down on your anger, and do not give the devil an opportunity." EPHESIANS 4:26-27 (NASB)

"Tremble and do not sin; meditate in your heart upon your bed, and be still." PSALM 4:4 (NASB)

Meditation

We duck our heads and run for cover when we hear a raised voice. We need three to four people to validate our opinions so we will have the courage to speak our minds. We may have been raised in a home where anger was considered "immoral."

Anger is a natural response to imposed wrongs or illegitimate behaviour. I'm talking about the kind of appropriate anger that can be used to empower a definition of "self."

Underlying the feelings of anger may be a deep fear of abandonment, the terror that someone will leave us if we speak our mind. Our "self" has such little definition that if someone left us, we feel that we would not exist. No one but God has the power over our lives to define who we are and what we were meant to be.

I was deeply involved in conversation with a young woman who said to me, "You don't get it; anger was immoral in the home where I grew up!"

"Yes, I get it," I told her. "It was in my home, too."

I can count on one hand the number of times I saw my father exhibit anger. My father, saint that he was, needed to get angry a few more times. In my opinion, I would have benefited if his indignation had led him to choose to act.

This young mother standing with me was articulate, intelligent, and emotionally normal. But for the life of her, she could not face down someone who was angry with her. Someone else's anger caused her to lose her thoughts and words, leaving her speechless. She was giving other people's anger power over her and her choices.

I lived in Seattle when Mount St. Helens erupted. Do you think Ms. Helens just vomited out of the blue? No, there were warnings and rumblings, but people who lived at the base refused to move. There were signs that Ms. Helens was getting ready to blow; when she did, she blew ashes on my car, four hours north of her!

The idea is not to store anger and eventually blow like Ms. Helens did.

We often feel terrified of our feelings of anger and we feel too vulnerable to express them. Unfortunately, unresolved anger doesn't disappear; our inner computer stores it in files for future use. After being stepped on enough, we may suddenly, without warning, "blow." Our anger may not land in the right place and can have damaging consequences.

The idea is to say what we need to say to the appropriate party when we need to say it. I feel the best about my words when I have thoughtfully shared my feelings of hurt and maintained my integrity of "self." It is the *way* I say what I say that matters. I can choose strength and self-control simultaneously.

"*Strong anxiety* inevitably is aroused when we begin to use our anger to define our own selves and the terms of our own lives more clearly. Some of us are able to start out being clear in our communications and firm in our resolve to change, only to back down in the face of another person's defensiveness or attempts to disqualify what we are saying" (*The Dance of Anger: A Woman's Guide to Changing the Patterns of Intimate Relationships*, by Harriet Lerner).

Anger itself is not "wrong." Anger is a God-given emotion that He Himself experienced. It is our misuse of it, however, that does not achieve His righteousness. But if anger is used appropriately, it can help define us. Anger is a clear message of how we feel. If we violate, negate, or invalidate anger, we will lose our sense of "self."

If we begin to talk about our repressed feelings of anger, this can threaten to change the balance of power in a relationship. We often misinterpret a person's anger for something other than what it is. Efforts may be wobbly at best to navigate the expression of angry feelings. We can learn to find meaningful ways to say what is on our minds.

Action Step

Buy time, if need be, to sort out your feelings. Remember that another's response does not determine whether you are right or wrong. You will have to know what you think and feel. Anger can be a temperature gauge, warning you of something inside. Each time you can risk saying what's inside, fear will lessen. Try to identify why you are angry and what precipitated the anger, and then learn to express your feelings appropriately.

Prayer

Lord, help me to buy time when I want to react. I know that if I react instantly without thinking, I might wish I'd said things differently. Give me strength to say what I need to say without the overstimulation of anger. I do not want to say angry words that hurt others and me.

My Journal

My Journal

Divine Travellers

Scripture

"Blessed be the God and Father of our Lord Jesus Christ, the Father of mercies and God of all comfort, who comforts us in all our affliction so that we will be able to comfort those who are in any affliction with the comfort with which we ourselves are comforted by God." II CORINTHIANS 1:3-4 (NASB)

Meditation

We were riding on Amtrak, travelling south from the San Joaquin Valley to southern California. I was rumbling along the tracks with my first cousin, with whom I had not spent any significant time in 30 years. I had stayed with her during the days of my mother's passing two months earlier.

In February 2007, I received a call from my mother's doctor. If I wanted to see my mother before she died, I needed to get in the car and come immediately. I threw a suitcase together and hit the road for the four-hour drive to the nursing hospital. I was exhausted that Thursday morning, trying to prepare for the mystery of my mother's departure. I arrived at the hospital, where I met my brother, and together we held vigil over our mother while she lay in a subdued and unresponsive state. All we could do was remain with her as a physical presence while the nurses provided care.

After four days in the hospital, I called my cousin and cried my eyes out. "I don't know what to do—she isn't dying. My family needs me at home and I'm spent on saying goodbye and being told this is her last breath." My cousin ran over with a plate of delicious toast and comforted me. Later that day, I left for lunch with my brother, and upon my return, I found my cousin singing hymns to my mother. It was transcendent. Early the next morning, around 4:00am, my mother left this world.

Several months later, my cousin and I pounded down the train tracks to my home. We had a chance to share the last 30 years through recollection. Growing up, I had always felt inferior to my cousin. She was known as the "Songbird." Her voice is a pure, natural, heavenly talent. She sang in every school play and church function and travelled on tour. I was skinny and untalented—so I thought. But the next four hours put our lives into perspective.

She shared her journey with me and I listened, glued to every word, thinking that I could have been more of a comfort to her along the way and her to me. I assumed that behind this Songbird voice was a Songbird whose life knew only success and pleasure. I was wrong. We dug deep into a well of vulnerability and authenticity in words. The miles that had kept us apart brought us home to each other's hearts.

I talked about my anxiety and she talked about her recovery from rejection. I found kindness, wisdom, honesty, and qualities that Songbirds learn to sing only in the dark, when no one knows they are singing. She became the serendipity of my spring during, and in the aftermath of, my mother's death. We acknowledged that if my mother had died quickly as presumed, we would not have locked lives for nine days.

By divine coincidence, her grown son lives near me, which has provided the good fortune of recurring visits. She has also helped me in my anxiety and depression during our regularly scheduled Saturday morning phone calls. She has understood depression, too.

I have met many divine travellers this past year. The experiences have been too profound to be coincidental. I have talked with people who suffer from depression in gas stations and Starbucks and have found myself in conversations on patios, in shops, and in the daily places of life. The topic of mental health has presented itself in many an unplanned conversation. I have found *angels unawares*. It takes time to find friends and to forge relationships. But the energy is much better spent this way than suffering in isolation, thinking we are alone.

Action Step

The toast my cousin brought that Monday morning before my mother died has been my morning breakfast for nearly a year. It's a small "covered dish." I thought I would share the recipe with you so while eating, you might remind yourself that there are those who care. Toast a slice of Ezekiel bread, butter to your liking,

spread with honey, sprinkle with cinnamon, and cover
with a layer of ground flax and berries.

Prayer

*Lord, help me to realize that I'm not the
only one who struggles with anxiety and
depression. Remind me that others who share
these struggles can bring great consolation.
Help me to reach out in comfort when I do not
feel I can. Help me not to believe the lie that I
am alone. This is a lie and not the truth. This
is the lie that makes me feel isolated. Protect
me from this kind of evil. Help me to believe
in the truth that You will never leave me or
forsake me. I am a child of God and I know
that You love me.*

My Journal

My Journal

Align with the Truth

Scripture

"So Jesus was saying to those Jews who had believed in Him, "If you continue in My word, then you are truly disciples of Mine; and you will know the truth, and the truth will make you free." JOHN 8:31-32 (NASB)

"Jesus said to him, 'I am the way, the truth, and the life; no one comes to the Father, but through Me.'" JOHN 14:6 (NASB)

"…but speaking the truth in love, we are to grow up in all aspects into Him who is the head, even Christ."
EPHESIANS 4:15B (NASB)

Meditation

When we do not know with whom, or with what, to align, we should align with the truth—the truth about ourselves, the truth about others, and the truth about God. This way, we can never lose.

People may ask us for allegiance and we may become confused. We consider why we are being asked to get "on board" as well as our motive for this allegiance. Allegiances and alignments without truth can become unhealthy, sticky, messy. But we can always align with the truth when we are unsure of what to do, and know that the truth will set us free.

The truth, however, can be frightening. Admitting truth about ourselves can produce anxiety; we may not be prepared to be honest. We may struggle deeply to come to grips with our truth. It doesn't mean that our truth trumps reality; it means that reality *becomes* our truth. Knowing the truth about someone else may mean that we have to address it.

We will be free from our old ways when we are willing to learn the truth about ourselves. We can let go of old lies. The closer we live to reality, the more mental health we will enjoy. Avoid denial; it does not serve us well. It only prolongs and deepens the grooves of our neuroses and addictions.

I have a distinct memory while growing up on a farm. We did not have the normal "amenities" of life. Our bathroom was small and served the four of us. One night, the light fixture in the bathroom ceiling was not working. My father placed a lamp on the toilet cover while he took a bath. When he got up from his bath, he absentmindedly grabbed the lamp and he lit up like a Christmas tree. I remember his shouts of struggle with this animal that clung to him; my mother had managed to get into the bathroom and was part of the battle with the lamp. I remember his final yell, somewhat like a shot putter, when he heaved the lamp from his grasp.

That's how difficult it will be for us to throw off our old ways of thinking. I recommend the book *The Language of Letting Go Journal* by Melodie Beattie (Hazelden, 2003). This can also be a daily help in heaving off old ways of participating in relationships in exchange for new ways that will bring freedom.

Action Step

Choose to be truthful with yourself and be kind and loving in the way you tell others the truth. Journal what you know to be true about yourself. When the enemy comes in to diminish your value, you can refer to what you have written. Identify what you know to be true about God from the Scriptures. This will be meaningful in times of turbulence. You know the plane will fly; this is just some rough air—it doesn't mean you're going down. You do not have to "white-knuckle" life when you remember that God is beneath you.

Prayer

Lord, help me to be truthful about myself in spite of how I will be received. Jesus stayed true to His purposes on earth. This is not easy; I need Your help to do this. There is always another pull inside my head. Others' reactions do not determine whether I have said the right thing. Help me to tell the truth.

My Journal

Feeling Left Out

Scripture

"And He also went on to say to the one who had invited Him, 'When you give a luncheon or a dinner, do not invite your friends or your brothers or your relatives or rich neighbours, otherwise they may also invite you in return and that will be your repayment. But when you give a reception, invite the poor, the crippled, the lame, the blind, and you will be blessed, since they do not have the means to repay you; for you will be repaid at the resurrection of the righteous.'"
LUKE 14:12-14 (NASB)

"Through all this Job did not sin nor did he blame God."
JOB 1:22 (NASB)

Meditation

Have you ever felt left out? I have. Sometimes I avoid people because I'm afraid of the anxiety of comparison that goes off in my mind. It's a terrible quicksand. Once I dangle my big toe in it, it sucks me in like the force of the best-made vacuum cleaner. This feeling of inferiority started at a very young age for me, and grew as I grew.

Rejoicing in meaningful events, passages discovered, and journeys treaded are the treasures that life gives us to celebrate. But when I hear a mother talk about her amazing brood of children, a couple share the exploits of their latest European travels and rave about their next trip to Rome, or someone brag about cramming people into his house for a wall-to-wall party, I feel left out. The shock of my own feelings of inferiority, which can leave me feeling paralyzed, comes as a recent surprise to me. I tend to wonder if God was passing out goodie bags and fell one short. There I stand, reaching out my hand, and nothing comes in return.

I think often we feel as though we are living "Plan B" for our lives, not Plan A. The road took a turn through no fault of our own or by choices we regret. I believe there are many "Plan B" people—people we've never met, people we bump into, people who fill our church pews each Sunday, people we know. They feel their lives are tarnished. They feel that no cleanser could rub their lives clean.

Why is the single individual who longs for marriage single? Why does the couple who aches for a baby infertile? Why does anyone born with a functional handicap face life with limitations? Why does the mystery of circumstance buy one a free ride while another can never see daylight? It's like a razor-sharp pain when we feel left out. It's such a relief when I find someone wearing, figuratively speaking, the exact same-sized shoes in which I have walked a mile. I don't feel so singled out, as if I were the object of God's punishment. It's a relief to know that I didn't set out to take the wrong trail.

My daughter drew a beautiful art piece of the poem *The Yellow Brick Road*; off to the top of the page, the road splits into eight or so destinations. There are numerous trail options. I thought it was magical to

behold. No particular trail was better than another
or the trail of choice easy to select. The Yellow Brick
Road does not always lead to the Land of Oz. In fact,
right next to the Land of Oz is the Land of Uz, where
spiritual conflict abounds and good people suffer bad
things. This is the land where well-meaning friends give
bad advice, where people feel abandonment and shame
for no particular wrongdoing, where we do not know
why we suffer. It is the land of Job.

Job was deserted by family and friends; they
concluded his suffering was because he had done
something bad. Quite to the contrary, he was a
righteous man who suffered *because* he was righteous.
This did not win him a popularity contest. I wonder if
Job thought he was living Plan B. . He sat in suffering
with no idea why. He was not privy to the conversation
God had with Satan.

When life does not make sense, we question our own
existence, as Job did his. A dear friend pointed out that
when things go wrong, we often blame God, not Satan;
the victim, not the perpetrator. I think it is interesting
that in all of Job's suffering, he did not blame God. We,
too, need to assign blame to the correct source.

The healing oil for combating this inferiority is
gratefulness and trust. In time, we will come to a place
of thankfulness and trust. These positive habits are
contrary to the negative habits of comparison. Through
prayer and practice, we will become more like the
person God intended us to be. It all has to do with
our ability to adjust the lens in our camera of life. We

might be far richer in things that really matter, but our impaired vision does not always allow us to see these riches.

I wonder whom Jesus would invite to dinner. We are on his guest list for the kingdom of God. Don't worry too much about those who sideline us here on earth. Remember, "the first shall be last and the last shall be first in his kingdom" (Matthew 20:16).

Action Step

Today, revel in those blessings for which you can thank God. Identify the blessings you have and the things you are able to do. You might be surprised at how much good you actually do, and have, despite how you feel.

Prayer

Lord, it is an awful feeling to see others do what I wish I could at times. This is hard for me. I feel like I wasn't a favored child. But you do not have favorites; You love me as much as You love others. Help me to be honest with You and talk to You about my needs and wants. Help me to identify the real blessings in my life. Help me to say, "Thank You."

My Journal

My Journal

Living with White Space

Scripture

"But we have this treasure in earthen vessels, that the surpassing greatness of the power may be of God and not from ourselves; we are afflicted in every way, but not crushed; perplexed, but not despairing; persecuted, but not forsaken; struck down, but not destroyed; always carrying about in the body the dying of Jesus, that the life of Jesus also may be manifested in our body." II CORINTHIANS 4:7-10 (NASB)

"Yet those who wait for the Lord will gain new strength; they will mount up with wings like eagles; they will run and not get tired, they will walk and not become weary." ISAIAH 40:31 (NASB)

Meditation

Being overwhelmed can trigger depression. Our bodies and brains weren't meant to handle so much. It is the convergence of multiple stressors that can trigger a depressive episode.

All too often, we take on far more than we are capable of handling. Women, in particular, who are natural caretakers and givers, tend to put themselves last. I recently read a document entitled "Margin," written by a friend and professional colleague. My friend was

asked to address the topic of burnout to a group of
overworked leaders. She told me it was one of her few
brilliant life moments; she had created a handout that
could only be read with a magnifying glass. The group
in front of her resorted to finding a reading lamp,
turning the page at different angles, adjusting their
reading glasses to bring it closer, or moving it farther
from their eyes. It took the group some time to realize
that the document itself illustrated, humorously, the
very issue about which she was speaking. These zealous
leaders were doing all the right things for all the right
reasons, but needed a supportive word to help them
honour balance. They needed to learn to live with "white
space," or margin, in their lives.

This past year of change in my life has taught me to
pay closer attention to my mental and emotional health.
People have told me that there is nothing they can cut
out of their lives. I have told myself this same lie. But
the unintended result is that our health and well-being
can be "cut out" if we try to do too much. Ultimately,
if we do not have our "self," what do we really have?
Saying, "No, I'm sorry, I can't do that" is an expression
of "self"—a loving act of self-care.

I find that anticipating cycles of energy output and
scaling back in preparation of it is helpful. I also find
it helpful to participate in activities that energize me,
such as entertaining, swimming, coffee with friends,
writing, and Friday nights off. God's creation is free
to be enjoyed. If we have to alter plans and reassess,
that is not a sign of failure, but an acceptance of our
limitations.

In the book *Protect Us from All Anxiety: Meditations
for the Depressed* (ACTA Publications, 1998), author

William Burke offers brief, daily thoughts on anxiety and depression as a result of coping with a period of time when he overextended himself.

In Christian circles, it is often considered "spiritual valour" to be overworked and underpaid. To work beyond our resources is often required; to work for nothing can be an expectation. However, overextending ourselves can lead to anxiety, depression, and suffering. There is no spiritual notch in the tree for overwork without remuneration. We are employees of Jesus Christ; he does not require overtime to get the job done. *He* is the one who will reward us for our work. Sometimes we will choose to give sacrificially of time and resources and other times, we will not. We need to accept this reality and let it be okay.

Action Step

What fills your tank with gas? Make daily Sabbaths. Enjoy moments of respite. Take your emotional pulse. Pay attention to your well-being. Protect yourself. Honor yourself and other things will fall into place, even if it means something must go. Quiet your anxiety long enough to enter into something that brings you pleasure; the more you try, the more it will be possible. Wait until panic has passed before you evaluate; nothing needs to be decided during panic. Breathe and slow your mental pace; things fall into place when we are taking life at a reasonable pace.

Prayer

*Lord, I need to refuel my tank. I need to live
at a pace that is congruent with my age and
health. I do not have the energy I used to
have. Help me to accept that reality and honor
my well-being.*

My Journal

My Journal

Enmeshment

Scripture

It was for freedom that Christ set us free; therefore, keep standing firm and do not be subject again to a yoke of slavery."
GALATIANS 5:1 (NASB)

Meditation

I vividly remember my brief stay in Wales. A few years out of college, I worked as a childcare worker at a conference for British and Welsh attendees. I, the American, along with a few others, offered my services to the parents so they could meet in peace. I was in charge of caring for several children in the group. One of my little girls had a noticeably obstinate attitude. I did my best to become her friend—I did not want a bad report to go home to her mother about the American caregiver.

On one particular afternoon, we took all the children for a stroll. The little girls wanted to bring their prams and baby dolls down the rocky path. I was trying to help this little girl gather her dolls and catch up with the group. At one point, she looked me dead in the eye and said, "My mummy said, don't you force me!" That ended that—we stayed back and played inside instead. I don't like to be forced to do things and neither did she.

Enmeshment, an unhealthy attachment to others, is like forcing other people to meet our needs. I think of it as flypaper. We can get stuck on it and have an almost impossible time escaping. Enmeshment is an easy slide. We may have felt disconnected and may have chosen this unhealthy attachment instead of facing the fear and challenges of being alone. When those we love distance themselves from us, we feel threatened and inclined to "lasso" them in at all costs. Enmeshed families have to work very hard to help each individual family member distinguish him or herself from the others, each having his or her own wants, needs, and desires.

"Homogenized," which means "all the same," is a good description on enmeshment. One of the places I've observed the phenomenon of enmeshment is Disneyland. I have watched families wandering about in herds. Did it occur to anyone to let everyone do his or her own thing and then meet back for dinner? It has always made me laugh to think that the "Happiest Place on Earth" is overrun by so many crying children. I've been there on hot, humid days with people sweating in their Mickey Mouse ears, waiting in two-hour lines for their favourite ride, spending hundreds of dollars on meals that sell outside for a fraction of the cost. It seems odd that this is meant to create happiness.

Family members that are enmeshed may feel as though they have to correct their emotions to please a relative. It is sort of like putting a sock in the mouth of emotions. But emotions need to be validated, not minimized. Everyone needs to be able to express an "emotional ouch" without repercussions or emotional punishment.

Real relationships involve giving others freedom in their choices. When we give people the freedom of choice to establish a relationship with us, they usually *want* to. The deeper the freedom, the deeper the love. God wants us to want him; otherwise, the relationship is not authentic. Being in any relationship—with friends, family members, spouses, God—should be a celebration of choice.

Action Step

Try to give people freedom to choose to be with you. State your need as it exists. If you need emergency help, let that be known, as well. Expect that people will give what they are able to give.

Prayer

Lord, help me to believe that people will give what they are able to give. I can only give from what I have. I sometimes live in disappointment because I attach unrealistic expectations to people I love. Lord, help me to free people to give what they can. Help me to give what I have in treasure, time, and talent.

My Journal

Walking on Glass

Scripture

"The thief comes only to steal and kill and destroy; I came that they might have life, and have it abundantly. I am the Good Shepherd; the Good Shepherd lays down His life for the sheep." JOHN 10:10-11 (NASB)

Meditation

When we are experiencing anxiety, depression, or addiction, we will hear many inaudible—but loud—voices. Those voices can say, "I do not deserve anything, I am worthless, all I do is mess up, I never know what to say, if I say anything it comes out all wrong, I'm so stupid, I never get anything right, no one is like me, I'm a mistake, I'm just a mess."

The voices will holler at us until we succumb. Yet we continue to smile and act as if everything is okay while there is a "civil war" going on in our mind. In fact, the split is as vast as the Grand Canyon. It is a terrible way to live. It appears to us that other people simply sit around, read books, and listen to music, yet we can't concentrate because of what's going on in our minds.

None of these voices is God's. None of these negative messages is from Him. The beginning of healing is aligning our negative self-talk with what we know to be true about what God says about us. Internalizing His value of us will help us combat those lies.

Peggy Claude-Pierre describes the "Confirmed Negativity Condition" in her book, *The Secret Language of Eating Disorders*. She describes "A Civil War in the Mind" through the voices of sufferers. Our minds have trouble with the entry and retrieving of information when we struggle with anxiety. Information never really gets stored in our long-term memory, because it does not make it's way completely into our memory and anxiety prevents us from retrieving this information when needed. We may feel like we are suffering from memory loss. This is very frustrating, but considered to be normal. One sufferer said, "My head feels like a war zone." This book stands as a tribute and a declaration of hope for the eating-disordered victim. If we make our way through the terror (of the personal accounts in her book) to the stories of recovery, we can exhale and realize that true recovery rings loud and clear as the path of hope for the suffering person. In order to move through depression and anxiety to freedom, the developmental life stages must start over and/or pick up where development stopped.

The constant personal barrage of internal disapproval leaves no room for positive external messages. Even the slightest hint of disapproval is interpreted as a threat. Information is interpreted through the grid of disapproval, which reinforces self-loathing. This leaves him or her resorting to deprivation and starvation in an attempt to replace and still the negative voices. And then, those around the victim believe they must behave in inauthentic ways to avoid threatening his or her survival. This is not merely "walking on eggshells"—it is "walking on glass." The victim will bleed, as will those around him or her.

Life is not about seeking perfection in relationships—it is not black and white. It involves meltdowns and stepping on toes because we did not see them under our feet in the first place. Shattering the perfection paradigm can create deep anxiety in our world. The smallest jostle implies the apocalypse. Our "negative mind" may seem larger than our body.

Action Step

Tell someone the qualities you love about them verbally or in writing. Provide a meal to someone or visit that person you think may be suffering. Jesus Christ said, "...*I tell you the truth, when you did it to one of the least of these my brothers and sisters, you were doing it to me!*" *(Matthew 25:40, NLT)*.

Prayer

Lord, You do not shame me for self-recrimination. I have always felt that You are the only one who understands this mental merry-go-round. Please protect me from self-hatred and replace those thoughts of self-loathing with Your value and love for me. Help me to stay close to people who protect my mind and heart.

My Journal

Happiness

Scripture

"These things I have spoken to you, so that in Me you may have peace. In the world you have tribulation, but take courage; I have overcome the world." JOHN 16:33 (NASB)

"Delight yourself in the Lord; and He will give you the desires of your heart. Commit your way to the Lord, trust also in Him, and He will do it." PSALM 37:4-5 (NASB)

Meditation

   Change it up! God does not want us to be miserable, stuck in the same rut. If we can change and/or improve our situation or circumstance, God is all for it. As a child, I was taught to adopt a "suffering theology." I thought my suffering was in alignment with God. However, and I know this may come as a complete shock, God wants us to wake up and be *happy*.
   I was speaking to an elderly lady at a hermitage I frequent. She told me that after the death of her husband, she remarried to a man who turned out to be a "control freak." Her son came to visit her and found his mother depressed beyond the point of recognition. He told her that she had the right to a happy environment for the rest of her life. Fortunately, the woman had

protected herself financially and found the courage to leave her overly controlling husband. Her son helped her move into a much happier living environment.

The hermitage is lovely and hidden in the busy city. The grounds are a horticultural miracle. The outer gardens are graced with a flowing stream and many birdhouses; the inner gardens have a large waterfall and a pool where ducks float and sunbathe. Tucked away in the back is a space where visitors enter and find solace. The simple desk, table, and kneeling bench create a sense of peace. I have left many prayer requests in the "God box," a box in which guests deposit their most secret, sacred written prayer requests. Nobody but God "sees" or "reads" these requests.

I have started my own "God box" at home. It sits on my desk and I frequently use it to deposit little prayer requests written on envelope edges or small pieces of paper. I know God does not forget, so I'm thankful that my short-term memory loss will not affect him.

We are the people of God's deep affection. He is concerned about us as well as our needs. Our continual accommodation of others and the suffering that comes from compromising our selves do not reflect his will. God supports the longings of our hearts. God dances in our delight. Why else would he say that if we delight in him, he will give us the desires of our heart? We can change it up in our lives by introducing involvements and relationships that bring us happiness; this is not "unspiritual." God has no "theology of misery" in mind for us. Jesus says reality will be inundated with trouble. So why add to it? Let's change it up for the better if we can!

Action Step

Create a "God box." Slip in a prayer request, as
needed. Let your God box grow. He says to ask and
receive that your joy may be full.

*"Until now you have asked for nothing in My name; ask
and you will receive, so that your joy may be made full"
(John 16:24, NASB).*

Prayer

*Lord, it is delightful that You delight in
me. You are continually creating special
indications that You know exactly how I'm
wired. It cheers me to know that You have
happiness in store for my life. Lord, help me to
slip in some "only-God-can" requests and wait
to see what You do.*

My Journal

Healing

Scripture

"The Lord will sustain him upon his sickbed; in his illness, You restore him to health." PSALM 41:3 (NASB)

"Truly, truly, I say to you, unless a grain of wheat falls into the earth and dies, it remains alone; but if it dies, it bears much fruit. He who loves his life loses it; and he who hates his life in this world will keep it to life eternal." JOHN 12:24-25 (NASB)

Meditation

My father lay in St. Agnes Hospital, still trying to put on an optimistic front. The doctor told him he was in the ninth inning of esophageal cancer. I had watched as the lab report indicated the pints of blood already lost through his system. I was there when the verdict of carcinoma of the esophagus was read.

My father was a "never-give-up" type of person. I tried to help him face reality. I remember him looking up at me and saying, "There are promises, you know," referencing the above verse in Psalms. The transfusions and attentive medical care, prior to radiation, gave him a glimmer of hope that God might heal his devastated body. God could have healed him, but my dad slowly left this earth over a nine-month period of intense physical suffering. His cancer was extremely advanced when diagnosed, so his chances of recovery were miniscule. If the cancer had been diagnosed when early warning signs had presented themselves, his prognosis would have been much better.

I relate this story because there is a connection between recognizing the early warning signs of anxiety and depression and one's rate of recovery. The earlier it is diagnosed and treated, the better the chances of healing.

The pursuit of healing in our emotional lives is similar to the pursuit of healing in our physical lives. However, it is not visible to the human eye, nor are there lab tests or exams with which to measure progress. The path of recovery may seem very uncertain. Our experience might seem like the end of emotional health while we are in the midst of anxiety and depression. However, this does not have to be the outcome. Hitting "rock-bottom" may even be just what we need to finally deal with our anxiety and depression.

I know I will never be free of anxiety, but like a chronic illness, it can be managed. Several things have helped me in the pursuit of my own healing. I can draw on coping skills, such as choosing to engage in an activity even though I do not feel like it, valuing myself enough to call a friend, attending to the responsibilities of daily chores, getting out of the house, heading to the YMCA for a swim, choosing prayer and Scripture-reading, learning to wait for the worst to pass, and allotting a small period of time for worry and then leaving my anxiety with God. When the anxiety is especially intense, the physical symptoms overtake my feelings. I have to choose to go into my mind and draw on my rational thinking.

Anxiety is also often situational, and I'm never sure what situation will sabotage me. I can gain a track record of coping and choose distractions and skills that will help me, despite how bad I feel. I have to *feel* to heal, and the feelings may not always be pleasant. However, unpleasant or awful feelings can be tolerated and understood. I'm convinced that when God exposes an area of wounding, his agenda is to heal it. If I'm laid out bare, it is purposeful. A.W. Tozer said, "God wounds us in our wounds." The very thing that seems our death shall become our life. The process will be as painful, ugly, and messy as surgery.

We mask pain in a variety of ways. We want to quell the pain quickly, so we may choose an addiction, a relationship, an extravagant vacation, money, or a new home in an effort to lessen the intensity of our discomfort. We hang on very tightly to destructive behaviours that create a false sense of security instead of turning to healing behaviours. I remember the day my therapist told me that I had an 80% chance of full recovery. He said that I might not even remember this major depressive episode; it may feel as though it did not happen. After healing from a ravaging illness, the memories can become dim if the symptoms are resolved. The scars may be reminders at times, but the illness may never ravage us again if the healing is in our favour.

I have to treat emotional illness as if it were a physical illness. What got me here has to "get fixed." It has been amazing to observe how my "cancer-recovery" friend and I compare similarities on the path of healing: Find the origin of the illness, identify the cause, seek treatment, and combine medicine and therapy. In the process, I may encounter doctors who are not experts in dealing with my diagnosis, but I will keep searching until I find the right doctor. I might choose to find a health advocate who will help me in my search. I will have good days and bad days. I will make progress and then take two steps backward. I will go into remission and wonder if I even had the disease. It may reappear, and I start over. What is crucial for me to remember is that I will pursue recovery *at all costs*. Participating in my healing and following doctors' orders significantly increases my chances of getting well.

Action Step

Take an active step toward healing. Seek help through a professional. Attempt to make an appointment with a practitioner who specializes in your diagnosis or addiction. Search through trusted friends for a good recommendation. View yourself as the consumer. *You* are the one looking for the right therapist or doctor. You do not have to please the professional. Participate in an intake appointment; if you do not feel it is a good match, keep enquiring and searching through the resources of your insurance provider or relational network. Do not give up until you have found some help.

Prayer

Lord, this side of heaven I may never truly be completely well, but I can pursue healing. I have to be an active participant with You. There are helpers who have studied and prepared to help. Guide me in my search for professional helpers. Help me to be brutally honest with the right doctors and therapists and act on what I learn. Reveal the truth of my struggles and help me to be willing to change.

My Journal

DAY EIGHTEEN

Risk-Taking

Scripture

"So then neither the one who plants nor the one who waters is anything, but God who causes the growth. Now he who plants and he who waters are one; but each will receive his own reward according to his own labor. For we are God's fellow workers; you are God's field, God's building."
I CORINTHIANS 3:7-9 (NASB)

"Therefore everyone who hears these words of Mine and acts on them, may be compared to a wise man who built his house on the rock. And the rain fell, and the floods came and the winds blew and slammed against that house; and yet it did not fall, for it had been founded on the rock."
MATTHEW 7:24-25 (NASB)

Meditation

   I want you to think with me about the journey of recovery. When I write recovery, I mean the recovery of "self." Any addiction or activity used as a numbing device to fight off pain can layer over our sense of "self." Regarding recovery, it is often better to focus on where we started rather than where we are now. We need to acknowledge and appreciate the progress we are making. It is so easy to think we have driven very little distance when, in fact, we've crossed state lines. We tend to think poorly of our efforts in recovery because our energy levels are low.

The Scriptural analogies of planting a garden and building a house as creative imagery can help you in your healing process. Think of recovery as somewhat like tilling a garden. Visualize a garden plot full of weeds with hardened soil—unfit for planting. If we start in one corner and begin to turn the soil, little by little we will work our way through the entire plot. We may realize that as we till the soil, the untended area behind us will allow weeds to pop up again. As we look back, we will think this isn't possible. How do we keep moving forward while making sure the soil behind us is freshly cultivated? The point is that it will never be as overgrown as when we first began. Recovery is a process of both moving forward and coming back to cultivate. It is an ongoing process that never really ends. One of the greatest agents for recovery is taking risks. Risk-taking is a sign of recovery. Trying something new is good for our psyches.

My grandfather was a carpenter and my father worked for him. I remember well the sound of nails being hammered into wood. If our goal is to build a house, we will have to get out our hammer and nails. If we hammer the same nail repeatedly, we will never erect a house. But if we learn a behaviour or a new relational skill, if we venture beyond our comfort zone, we'll have hammered in a new nail. Our building will be completed in its own time; we are not in a contest with the Jones' family next door. This is *our* house and *our* garden; we can make them as unique as we choose. We will grow and build at our own pace, which is often in "baby steps." The good news is we can always start over. At the core, recovery will never be the same as when we first started; it is an evolutionary process. We can always go back to the beginning, to the time when we said, "I will pursue recovery at all costs."

"Settling" is an important concept for those of us who struggle with anxiety and depression to understand. We settle when we stop reaching for more, stop reaching for a higher goal, or when we stifle our own wishes and desires because of someone else's habits or forces. In recovery, we often settle for the wrong reasons. When do we honour boundaries and when do we settle? If we settle for the wrong reasons, we can shrink our world smaller than God intended. In recovery, we learn when to risk and when to stand at ease and we grow to discern the difference between the two. God does not intend for us to shrink our worlds. For example, we may notice our chronic illness is incrementally worsening, so we either give up or push harder and exercise more, thereby continuing to risk. Or, we become aware of our tendency to isolate from people, so we either accept our "fate" or risk involvement in relationships so we don't have to settle for becoming more of a recluse. This discernment process is part of our recovery. Settling versus risk-taking is part of it. Our minds, like our bodies, atrophy when we don't use them.

Action Step

Identify steps of wellness. What risks have you recently taken? How do you feel about the risk taken? What did you learn from it? Was it something you tried to say to someone? Was it participating in a new activity? Was it taking a job interview? Was it travelling to a new destination? Was it choosing to drive the freeway instead of surface streets? Was it departing with "stuff" that you know your U-Haul will not take to heaven? Was it confronting a phobia? What risks might you try? Who can help you try something new? If you enter a new involvement, you will grow, which will promote recovery!

Prayer

Lord, help me not to habituate to my circumstances. I want to go and grow until the day I die. It is easy to get into ruts and give up on trying. Help me to take risks, meet new people, try new things, go new places. Please give me the confidence I need to try these new things. Give me confidence to ask others to help me accomplish my dreams.

My Journal

My Journal

Bucket Friends

Scripture

"Therefore, humble yourselves under the mighty hand of God, that He may exalt you at the proper time, casting all your anxiety upon Him, because He cares for you. Be of sober spirit; be on the alert. Your adversary, the devil, prowls about like a roaring lion, seeking someone to devour. But resist him, firm in your faith, knowing that the same experiences of suffering are being accomplished by your brethren who are in the world." I PETER 5:6-9 (NASB)

Meditation

Our friends spent time in Nairobi, Kenya. The husband was recruited to teach in a business school and the wife assisted African women in designing art and crafts to sell and provide for their families. My friend has this amazing art flair. There are stencils on the walls of her high ceilings and at holiday time, everything glimmers in beautiful colours. This intersection with the Nairobi women was literally tailor-made for her.

She shared a story about the women she taught. The women exchanged scarves as a symbolic gesture for carrying each other's burdens. For example, if a mother was a single parent or had an ill child, she gave a scarf to another woman, requesting her to carry the burden for her.

The important role close friends play in each other's lives is conveyed in this short conversation between a young bride and her mother; it is entitled "Sisters", and the author is anonymous. The young bride held a glass of iced tea while she and her mother chatted on the porch. The mother unsuspectingly advised her daughter to always remember her sisters. "Remember that 'sisters' means all the women…your girlfriends, your daughters, and all your other women relatives too. It sounded strange at the time because she was joining the "couple's world." But as the hourglass of life slowly drained, she gradually came to understand that her Mom really knew what she was talking about. As time and nature work their changes and their mysteries upon women, sisters are their mainstays of life." The wise mother advises her newly married daughter to always remember her "sisters," even though she is now married. "Remember that 'sisters' means all the women [in your life]…your girlfriends, your daughters, and all your other [female] relatives, too," the mother explains. The daughter didn't realize, at first, the importance of this advice, but as the hourglass of life slowly drained, she gradually came to understand that her mother really knew what she was talking about. She had come to depend on the other women in her life—her mother, sisters, daughters, girlfriends, other female relatives— even well into her married years. "As time and nature work their changes and their mysteries upon women, sisters are their mainstays of life," writes this author.

My husband affectionately calls my girlfriends "The Posse"—and they truly are. They are scattered geographically but bound in heart through me. These women have been the mainstays of my life recently and in the past, as well. It is my dream to bring them all together and introduce them to each other; we could share the scarves of our lives, much like the scars of our lives. These women have been my blanket in the cold, my "bucket friends."

Buckets from the old days were made of wooden staves—vertical wooden slats that were typically wrapped horizontally by a metal ring. In a worn-out bucket, one or more slats might become broken. I believe that we only "hold water" (or have health) to the lowest stave. If all the other staves are high, but one is only two inches tall, the bucket will only hold two inches of water. How might a bucket hold *more* water? One (obvious) option is to heighten the lowest stave. Instead, let me suggest the concept of putting a larger, stronger bucket under the broken bucket, allowing the broken bucket to hold water to the capacity of the outside bucket. In the same way, "bucket friends" surround us and hold us up when we are unable to hold ourselves up.

Action Step

Identify the "bucket friends" in your life. Continue to strengthen and deepen your relationships with trusted friends. This will contribute to reducing anxiety and depression and shrinking the enemy of isolation—the enemy who prowls about, "seeking someone to devour."

Prayer

Lord, thank you for my friends! They are treasures and jewels. Help me to be a good friend, too. I know there is a wealth of healing friends available, but I have to reach out. Help me to tell my friends how much they mean to me and to treat them with love and respect. Give me the courage to interact with others, even when I am afraid.

My Journal

A Drowning Lifeguard

Scripture

"When Jesus then saw His mother and the disciple whom He loved standing nearby, He said to His mother, 'Woman, behold, your son!' Then, he said to the disciple, 'Behold, your mother!' and from that hour the disciple took her into his own household." JOHN 19:26-27 (NASB)

"For my father and my mother have forsaken me. But the Lord will take me up." PSALM 27:10 (NASB)

Meditation

Mothers and their children are bonded for life, no matter what life stage they are in, no matter how the relationship changes. Although motherhood changes as the transitional passages change for their children, mothers often try to maintain the same role they did when their children were under their care, rather than letting go. A professor of psychology once told me that the role of a mother is never finished because mothers are *always* caregivers.

If we think of the mother of Christ, there is evidence of her changing role and the intuitive knowledge she had about her son—Jesus—that no one else possessed. It was Mary who begged for his first miracle (John 2:3-

10). It was Mary who had a gut sense of his destiny that she could not comprehend. At his birth, "she pondered all these things and treasured them in her heart" (Luke 2:19). This is the same mother who experienced the independence of Jesus when his earthly family came to retrieve him, and he chose to follow God's purpose and identify followers as his family, too.

At times, mothers have to tolerate watching their children suffer. The unthinkable sometimes happens to devoted mothers—alienation, untimely death, suffering. *When I Lay My Isaac Down* is a book about the profound story of a mother's grief over her son's incarceration following his choice to murder. My friend wrote *Mother Held Hostage* and in it details the journey of her son, John, and his battle with Tourette syndrome, culminating in his suicide.

Mary, the mother of Jesus, had to endure the unthinkable. The mother of Jesus peered up at her son in human flesh and watched as those who crucified him stuck a sponge of sour wine in his blood-soaked mouth. In the moments following, Christ cried, "It is finished!" (John 19:30). Because Mary was the mother of the Son of God, it doesn't mean that she felt any less pain than any other mother would have felt in her place. Even though she knew her son's unique role in history, this did not lessen the pain of that loss. Mary had inclinations of this for years. She knew that she had given birth to God's Son. She knew that Jesus was not the result of a traditional human union.

The pain associated with having a child doesn't end when the labour is over—it is lifelong. Sometimes, the Bible portrays God with traits of motherhood as he relates to his children, the Israelites. He bears with them and carries them and nurtures them.

Several mothers have said to me, "I've never told anyone" regarding their child's journey. They don't talk at church. Mothers look perfect and respectable, but who would know their pain? My friend told me to picture myself placing my child in a basket going up to Jesus, leaving the child in the basket, knowing that God's love is so much greater than my own capacity to love. The Lord will always carry his children.

My friend's son was a lifeguard. He told his mom that when rescuing a drowning person near the pilings of a pier, the lifeguard is instructed to keep the drowning person between the leg of the pier and him or herself. Why? If there are two drowning people, one cannot save the other. On an airplane, we are instructed to bring the oxygen mask to our own face before helping someone else. Our recovery is as important, or *more* important, because it represents the hope for others' survival, as well. We must thrive, no matter their choices.

Action Step

Take a step in your own recovery. Make self-care an important priority. Attend to your journey and needs. Bring your prayers to God. Ask Him for help to be present, the ability to let go, and for the wisdom to

know the difference. Seek the counsel of mothers whom
you admire.

Prayer

*Lord, "letting go" may be one of the hardest
things for a parent to do. I do not even know
how to do it, but I need and want to learn.
Help me to let my child take her turn at bat
and not get in the way. Help me to let her
individuate from me. Lord, help me to believe
that You can take care of her. Meet her needs
in ways that I can never know. Give me
wisdom for her adult transition.*

My Journal

My Journal

Things Are Not as They Appear

Scripture

"And those members of the body which we deem less honorable, on these we bestow more abundant honor, and our less presentable members become much more presentable, whereas our more presentable members have no need of it. And if one member suffers, all the members suffer with it; if one member is honored, all the members rejoice with it."
I CORINTHIANS 12:23, 24A, 26 (NASB)

Meditation

A commercial shows a group—rather, a crowd—of people representing friendship. Someone in the crowd is labelled with mental illness. The number of friends still standing by the mental illness-labelled person progressively dwindles to zero. It makes me sad to watch and to realize that the stigma attached to mental illness may minimize human connection for the sufferer.

A friend once asked me, "Do you know when you have been kissed by God? You have been kissed by God when you are authentic and not *judged*." Jesus said, "Do not judge lest you be judged" and James wrote, "Mercy triumphs over judgment."

Things are not always as they appear. A well-known preacher was addressing an audience at a large conference. He was preaching as he so eloquently had in the past. As he spoke, he noticed a man sitting in the front row, nodding off and appearing inattentive. This preacher lost some of his focus but was able to complete the message. Afterward, the woman accompanying the man approached the preacher and apologized for her husband's struggle. The woman told the preacher that he was undergoing chemotherapy and that she brought him to church that morning in the hopes that he would find encouragement in the message. The preacher immediately withdrew his ill-formed conclusion of what appeared to be this man's disinterest.

This story has made an indelible impression on me. Now, when I look into people's eyes, I'm not sure I'm seeing the "whole truth and nothing but the truth." I do not know their fight of faith, their personal struggles, their private pain. I do not know their true capabilities. My judgment and God's judgment may be very different; ultimately, God's judgment is what matters. Jesus said, "Beware when all men think well of you." On the road to recovery, we will have to give up the continual wondering, "What will they think of me?" As Henri Nouwen has said, "Stop measuring your value by the yardstick of others."

The perfect inscription for the front door of my childhood home would be, "What will they think of us?" This was the ultimate value that drove our choices and behaviours. The "honour and shame" culture in which I grew up governed much of what I said and did. Over time, I came to realize that it does not matter what "they" think of us. "They" do not have the information "they" need to form an opinion of us. It might be interesting to take an internal pulse of how another's opinion factors into our decisions. We need to examine our decision-making process. Do we make decisions solely based on the notion of either pleasing or displeasing others?

Action Step

Be mindful of what you conclude about others. You lack the whole picture. Take some time to really get to know the people around you.

Prayer

Lord, things are not as they appear. I cover my hurt, just as others do. Help me not to judge. My life is the only life for which I can be responsible. Help me to stay in my own yard and not look over the fence into another's. Help me to bring words of healing to those who are hurting.

My Journal

Your Job: Get Well

Scripture

"Come to Me, all who are weary and heavy-laden, and I will give you rest. Take My yoke upon you, and learn from Me, for I am gentle and humble in heart; and you shall find rest for your souls. For My yoke is easy and My load is light."
MATTHEW 11:28-30 (NASB)

Meditation

Can we imagine the job of getting well? Can we imagine being hired? How fast would it take us to fill out an application? How early would we be at HR?

I sincerely believe if a company started by collecting people and underwriting their healing, the company would eventually become a Fortune 300, if not 100. Forbes would write amazing things about the newest and most innovative business plan ever imagined.

My writing is about the internal anatomy of depression. What is it *really* like on the inside? When do we know it is time to ask for help? Psychologically, I experienced it as an inability to get traction. We used to shove farm implements out of ditches and gullies when I was growing up. Sometimes, the tractor simply was stuck in the mud to stay. No matter the force behind it, it wasn't going to move forward. Just like the tractor, we can feel paralyzed in our depression and anxiety.

There we go, and no matter what we do with the pick of our ice skates, we continue to slip and slide. We may feel that our mind is slipping and sliding on us. Sometimes, the only way to get back up from the ice on which we have fallen is to *STOP* and get help.

Another picture that comes to mind is of someone treading water in a swimming pool. We expend all this energy and get nowhere. In these situations, we need a "heave-ho" from behind or a hand to reach in and pull us out of the pool. That is often what rest provides. If we psychologically stop long enough, we may regain strength and energy.

According to a therapist friend of mine, physical symptoms of a major depressive episode could include insomnia, hyper-somnia, fatigue, significant weight loss or gain, a chronic depressed mood, diminished pleasure in all or almost all activities, feelings of worthlessness, psychomotor agitation, excessive guilt, and possible suicidal thoughts and/or attempts. Such symptoms deserve immediate medical attention.

We may experience fluctuation in our recovery. We may improve on Friday evening, and then hit the floor on Sunday night when we have to face the responsibilities of the week. We may feel better in the evening, and then feel "stuck" in the morning. There tends to be a correlation between the amount of structure in our lives, or lack thereof, and our level of anxiety.

We can assign a number to our anxiety level, with "1" being the least anxious and "10" being extremely anxious. Then, we can monitor the anxiety fluctuation with corresponding activities or lapses in recovery. In my case, Mondays are seemingly worse than other times because they correlate with a time of extreme anxiety. Mondays have a psychological correlation of severe "mind pain" for me. Your specific triggers will be different. So what can we do? We can become a student of our "selves" and help unlock the door that leads to recovery. For example, it is very important for me to create structure on Mondays, which helps me cope with the anxiety.

A woman shared with me about how her husband told her not to worry about money or the house. He wanted her to focus on getting well. This woman has been out of work and worries that she is not contributing financially to the household. But the longer she is out of work, the more fearful she is of re-entering the workforce—she feels safe cocooning in her home. She is also a food addict, turning to food for comfort, which has turned into a lifelong battle with her weight. As her anxiety level increases, so do the numbers on the scale.

There are wounds she needs to deal with in order to heal her addiction. There are wounds we all need to deal with in order to heal our addictions. The need to deal with core wounds is often related to our present behaviours.

Action Step

Make it your job description to get well, emotionally and mentally. Draw up a job description of what that is. Just like you would be given a job description by an employer, make it your assignment to get well.

Prayer

*Lord, I desire to learn from You.
You understand my internal pain. You invite
me to come to You for rest. You promise Your
load is light. You invite the weary and heavy-
laden. I am one of those. I come to You for
relief and healing. Heal me, Lord Jesus.*

My Journal

My Journal

My Yard, Your Yard

Scripture

"But speaking the truth in love, we are to grow up in all aspects into Him, who is the head, even Christ."
EPHESIANS 4:15 (NASB)

Meditation

The above verse is a string of pearls out of a treasure chest in the fourth chapter of Ephesians. My dear friend has this saying: "My yard, your yard." It's acknowledging the personal boundary markings of another's thoughts, words, and choices. Imagine a fence with a gate that has hinges that can be used to open our degree of authenticity with others. We can always be honest, but we choose *degrees* of openness.

The level of earned relationship bears an important role in speaking the truth with others. The relationship has earned the right to speak in my life. Rarely do my friends "correct" me, because they have their own yards to maintain. How can I really maintain my yard when I'm busy weeding someone else's?

It says in *The Chronicles of Narnia* that the lion Aslan (symbolizing Jesus) someday will ask you about *your own* journey. He will not ask you about your neighbour's journey, your best friend's journey, your spouse's journey, your parents' or your children's journey—just yours. That's why we can only be responsible for our own yard. We are also responsible for those whom we let into our yard. Would we let just *anyone* come into the yard that surrounds our home? Of course not! The same holds true in our personal lives—not everyone is welcome.

My friend recently wrote me the following words: "Remember, you are only responsible for 'your yard;' i.e., your own choices, your own beliefs, your own perceptions, and your own feelings. As you interact with your loved ones, remember that they, too, have been given their own yards to cultivate and manage." We often take responsibility where we have no control. It is very tiring to work in someone else's yard. If we choose to do so, we may get involved in things that are none of our business and we may take on more responsibility than we can handle.

Relationship earns the privilege to speak. It is very clarifying for me when my friend asks me if she can come into my yard with her perceptions; it differentiates me from her, and helps me think my own thoughts and recognize them apart from hers.

The book of Job has taken on special meaning for me because, in the end, Job's friends were rebuked for insisting that Job's suffering was a result of sin. *The Life Recovery Bible* says the following: "There will always be people like Elihu, who think they have all the answers. They will give us reasons for our actions and condemn our lifestyle, thinking that wisdom has been given to them alone. But we need to be careful about listening to these people. We need to consider: 1) Do they have our best interests at heart? 2) Do their words build us up or tear us down? 3) Is what they are saying from God? If any of these questions can be answered 'no,' then they are not the people to help us in the recovery process. Elihu meant well, but his words, like those of Job's other three friends, did little to help Job cope with his suffering."

Action Step

Determine if you are spending unnecessary time working in someone else's yard. Changing someone else is an impossible task. You can only change yourself and your own behaviours. It may be a relief to know you are not responsible *for* others, only responsible *to* them. You cannot govern their change.

Prayer

Lord, I can only change myself with Your help. It is a relief that I do not have to busy myself trying to "fix" someone else. I forget that. I worry so much about others, as though I can be a "savior." Help me to let go, trusting that You love and care for those I do. I give my loved ones to Your care.

My Journal

Indecision-Making

Scripture

"But if any of you lacks wisdom, let him ask of God, who gives to all generously and without reproach, and it will be given to him. But he must ask in faith without any doubting, for the one who doubts is like the surf of the sea, driven and tossed by the wind. For that man ought not to expect that he will receive anything from the Lord."
JAMES 1:5-7 (NASB)

"And do not be conformed to this world, but be transformed by the renewing of your mind, so that you may prove what the will of God is, that which is good and acceptable and perfect."
ROMANS 12:2 (NASB)

"We are destroying speculations and every lofty thing raised up against the knowledge of God, and we are taking every thought captive to the obedience of Christ."
II CORINTHIANS 10:5 (NASB)

Meditation

We may feel like a deer in the headlights when it comes to making decisions. Our minds go down this path and then that path and we end up in a roundabout.

Circling, circling, even little daily decisions get us stuck in a cul-de-sac.

Indecisiveness is both a cause and a symptom of anxiety and it is one of the most painful and frustrating. This is when drawing on cognitive resources, such as thinking rationally to the best of our ability, is vital. It is often helpful to identify where our thinking is clogged. Like a clogged drain, our thinking can sometimes become stuck or paralyzed and we need something to help the drain flow freely. What decisions have held us hostage? Are there choices we can make that will help create movement again?

At times, we may abdicate and let a decision be forced for the sheer relief of not having to make a decision. However, it is better to make decisions, without the goal of being perfect, than it is to abdicate. This will guarantee periods of serious anxiety, yes, but they will pass. Pleasing others is often at the core of our inability to make decisions. Sometimes, the inaction is the fear of being truthful with ourselves and releasing the fear of making a mistake. A decision can be weathered and pondered without panic. Our spirit might be crushed, but our brain is not broken; our mind is a gift from God. We can still make good decisions, even under the worst of circumstances.

Buying time is a good practice; we can take the time to reason. That's how God sets us apart from the animal kingdom. God gives us the ability to reason and think things through objectively. The more we can grow our objective "self," the less likely anxiety will surface and drag us through irrational scenarios and vain imaginings.

Anxiety is not "true north." ~~It interferes with our~~ ~~ability to know if we are going in the right direction.~~ Anxiety may cause our stomachs to churn and turn. Living in seasons of uncertainty may aggravate our most uncomfortable feelings. Under these conditions, we can rely on rational powers to help us make a decision. It is better to make a decision and fail than to make no decision at all.

I was raised with the idea that God was narrow-minded—that he had only one, very specific path for me to follow. I thought I was playing hide and seek with his will. I was counting, God was hiding, and it was my job to find him. I had become a theological pretzel when it came to making decisions; I always had to do the "right" thing but kept seemingly missing the mark. . . Psalm 139 makes it very clear that there is nowhere God is not. Life has so many gray areas; situations are not always that black and white. In God's eyes, I had a lot of room to experiment, but I just didn't realize that. I could start down a path and then decide I'd rather change to another.

I just read the following passage from *Streams in the Desert*, a favourite devotional book my father passed along to me. The following is one of my favourite entries (August 20): "There comes a crisis-hour to each of us, if God has called us to the highest and best, when all resources fail; when we face either ruin or something higher than we ever dreamed; when we must have infinite help from God and yet, ere we can have it, we must let something go; we must surrender completely;

we must cease from our own wisdom, strength, and righteousness, and become crucified with Christ and alive with him. God knows how to lead us up this crisis, and he knows how to lead us through."

There is a difference between wanting to go in the right direction and wanting to go your *own* way, without considering God and others.

Action Step

Make a list of decisions you must make. Make a list of the pros and cons of these decisions. Then, reason it through and make the best decision you can with what you know. It actually has proven to be a very helpful cognitive tool. Remember: we can only do the best we can.

Prayer

Lord, why is it so hard to make decisions? I surrender my will to Yours as a start. I intend to follow You. Give me strength to decide. You have promised to help me with decisions without reminding me of my faults. I have to use the mind You gave me and trust that my mind is a gift for life. Help me to respect my thoughts and ideas.

My Journal

My Journal

Zero Visibility

Scripture

"Without consultation, plans are frustrated, but with many counsellors they succeed." PROVERBS 15:22 (NASB)

Meditation

I grew up in the San Joaquin Valley, the heart of "tule fog" land. The fog was so thick for much of the winter that there was zero visibility when looking out the car window. I have a couple of vivid memories of those winters. During high school, we took school buses to off-site football games. The buses were packed with noise and restless kids. Gloves, coats, and knee socks kept us warm while the prospect of cheering our team on kept us moving in our seats. While the bus was in motion, the chaperones (teachers or coaches) stood on the front steps of the bus with the door open. It was their job to watch for the side of the road and instruct the driver to stay on the road. If they weren't there to guide the driver through the fog, we might have ended up in a ditch or veering into oncoming traffic.

After my college years, I recall my brother picking me up on a return trip from Seattle. We were driving on the freeway at a snail's pace because of the dense fog. We thought it was curious to see headlights that seemed to be coming directly at us. We quickly pulled off and realized we were on the wrong side of the freeway! That's how thick the fog was.

Sometimes, in our journey of life, our vision will become significantly compromised. The fog will become very thick, our conclusions may become distorted, and we will not be the best judge of our own wellness. Let's say I'm a cancer patient and I go to the doctor and tell her I'm feeling particularly well, so chemotherapy will not be necessary. Then I might rattle on about my current symptoms. The doctor would inform me of the desperate nature of my condition and it would not matter what I thought about my treatment. My prognosis for recovery would be significantly reduced if I were left to my own devices.

We should expect that there will be "tule fog" in our lives. We will be driving on the wrong side of the freeway and not even realize it. The best advantage we have is depending on the perspective of those who understand our particular dilemma and let them speak. For a time, we will need to rely on those who have a better grasp of our ultimate well-being, even if it seems contrary to what we think may be best. They are not there to *control* us, but to *help* us. However, in the journey of wellness, it is difficult to give up control and trust in others.

Action Step

Identify several people you can trust to turn to in times of need for perspective. They won't be able to "do life" for you, but may have an honest opinion that might be important to take into consideration.

Karen
Troy
Jan

Prayer

Lord, I cannot always see my way down the path of life. There are hills and valleys and, at times, I have to walk in the valleys. I need others' help. Help me not to be embarrassed to ask for help in times of need. Help me to lock arms with those whom I trust and ask them to pray for me.

My Journal

Push Through

Scripture

"For if you cry for discernment, lift your voice for understanding; if you seek her as silver, and search for her as for hidden treasures, then you will discern the fear of the Lord, and discover the knowledge of God." PROVERBS 2:3-5 (NASB)

"Ask, and it shall be given to you; seek, and you shall find; knock, and it shall be opened to you. For everyone who asks receives, and he who seeks finds, and to him who knocks it shall be opened. Or what man is there among you who when his son asks him for a loaf, will give him a stone? Or if he asks for a fish, he will not give him a snake, will he?" MATTHEW 7:7-10 (NASB)

Meditation

I was standing between the pilings of the pier one afternoon, listening to the pounding of the surf. It reminded me of having a fetal doppler on my stomach during my pregnancy and hearing the methodical, rhythmic pound of my daughter's heart; it was music to my ears. The surf methodically rose and fell and the waves crashed against the pilings and rushed to the shore. The longer I stared at the end of the pier, the more I began to see a distant window of light. Through the pilings and rising surf, the window presented itself as a perfectly shaped square. The scene before me was infused with rushing and roaring, contrasted with the window-of-light-calm beyond the surf. The ocean levelled squarely with not a hint of drama. As I stared, I realized I was staring at a window of hope.

Unanticipated traumas can make us feel as though we are swimming desperately between the pilings, sucking in air and coming up for breath. The only thing to do is look for the "square" of light.

While strolling the beach promenade weeks later, I came upon various artists selling their wares. To my astonishment, I found a painting of the scene I just described. The artist had entitled it "Tunnel Vision," and it was painted after his 30-year battle with depression. My photo represented the hope the artist gained by peering through the pilings and looking beyond the drama of the sea.

Today, I thought about *pushing through* in life. We don't always get the things we want easily; it usually involves struggle! It is a fact that a baby bird's hatching process—the struggle and pushing to be set free from the shell—is what gives it life. If we were to interfere with the process, the bird would die. If, in sympathy, we were to assist the baby bird in breaking its shell, the struggle that creates life would be eliminated. The struggle *is* life. Our struggle between the pilings is God's way of giving us life.

Pushing through during depression and anxiety can be very cathartic. We may have no feelings on which to draw, but choosing productivity will promote healing. Repeatedly engaging in constructive activities can become a way of life, even without the desire to do so.

Daily chores and responsibilities will provide a sense of betterment, despite periods of inaction. We might ask ourselves, "Will we feel better after we accomplish this task?"

Action Step

Identify the pilings in your life. Elevate them to a place of prayer and contemplate *pushing through*. What can you do today that you do not feel like doing? **Push through and the rewards will come!**

Prayer

Lord, I do not always feel like others understand how much more I have to push through to get to the next step. I do not have good feelings to do what I need or want to do. Help me to push through and wait for the happiness to come after I complete my chore. Give me strength to push through without good feelings and to wait for the rewards.

My Journal

Fear

Scripture

"Do not fear, for I am with you; do not anxiously look about you, for I am your God. I will strengthen you, surely I will help you, and surely I will uphold you with My righteous right hand." ISAIAH 41:10 (NASB)

"And I say to you, My friends, do not be afraid of those who kill the body and after that have no more that they can do. But I will warn you whom to fear; fear the One who, after He has killed, has authority to cast into hell; yes, I tell you, fear Him!" LUKE 12: 4-5 (NASB)

Meditation

I was sitting on the veranda of the old Olympic Village in Hungary, where I was staying for a national conference with a mission's organization for which I served as staff. I was talking to a therapist who had come from the U.S. to volunteer his time and services. I remember nothing about that conversation, but I did not forget his name or where he was from.

The sights and sounds of Budapest are still very real in my mind. The gardens that provided the vegetables for each home looked colourful and the McDonald's that stood alone in our village provided a thumbprint of North America.

Some years later, I decided to connect with the therapist I met in Budapest—he was local enough for me to visit. Reflecting on our therapeutic process together, I can identify one recurring theme: facing my fear. However, "facing my fear" was more like moving toward my fear, going into it, chasing it down, daring it, confronting it, saying, "Bring it on!" I was very frightened by the prospect of what lay ahead of me. However, I faced my fears and sought treatment. It has been an arduous journey, taking me over many hills and into many valleys. Because I risked facing my fears and doing the difficult work required, I have experienced the hope of recovery. A friend said to me recently, "I've always thought of the Christian life as a progressive climb, but I'm beginning to think of it more in terms of scaling mountains and repelling into valleys."

Franklin Roosevelt said, "There is nothing to fear but fear itself." Fear has stopped more progress in the world than any other force on the planet. It has stopped my progress, too, hung up in the noose of fear. We may feel as though we have been arm-wrestling with fear our entire lives; sometimes we are stronger than the fear, and other the times the fear is stronger than we are. I have learned that it is imperative to move *toward* my fear, not run from it. Otherwise, it will chase me down and become bigger and bigger. It has a way of taking on a life of its own and morphing into a monster! The therapist whom I'd met in Budapest told me that 80% of what we fear never happens. Our fears hold us in bondage!

In the Scriptures, I counted more than 30 times that God says to people, "Do not fear." God knew that we would be very fearful beings. ~~Those who confronted the unexpected were reassured;~~ those who were given a new assignment were doubly assured. Moses got so tongue-tied that God had to accommodate his fear by giving him a spokesperson, sort of like a press secretary.

Fear is one of the most common experiences of the human existence. We may avoid going places or doing things that would benefit us because we are afraid. That is such a loss, and is no way to live our lives. I have learned that it is essential to enter the closet of fear; often, we find there is no "boogie man" hiding in there. Running toward fear, not away from it, is the only way to conquer fear.

Action Step

Write a page on what you fear the most and see if you are surprised with what unfolds. Listen to Jesus' words: *"...I will never fail you. I will never abandon you"* *(Hebrews 13:5, NLT).*

Prayer

Lord, I am afraid. I'm afraid of catastrophe as well as the small surprises that I hoped would not happen. I'm just a sheep in Your pasture. I'm defenseless without You. You have given me Your ever-present Word and Your Spirit to guide me. God, be my fence of protection. Help me to reflect on my safety in Your care. You guard me.

My Journal

Getting Slimed

Scripture

"What then shall we say to these things? If God is for us, who is against us? He who did not spare His own son, but delivered Him up for us all, how will He not also with Him freely give us all things? Who will bring a charge against God's elect? God is the one who justifies; who is the one who condemns? Christ Jesus is He who died, yes, rather who was raised, who is at the right hand of God, who also intercedes for us." ROMANS 8: 31-34 (NASB)

Meditation

I know you—you are slimed in guilt; the gelatinous green slime of guilt has enrobed you. You not only feel guilt; you feel *excessive* guilt to the point of being paralyzed. It's as though you have taken on the sins of the whole world. Your depression talks to you through guilt. You have taken responsibility for not only yourself, but also for the destiny of others.

You already feel like you are "taking" from the planet by your mere existence. You have "Need" written on you with a capital "N." You don't feel worthy—you feel you don't deserve a parking space. It's as if you wanted to get inside the mall, but you never even park your car. Your guilt slimes you; the messages that it imposes on you slime you. You want to move forward, but you can't. Your negative self-talk has you beaten down into the ground. You hear a voice in your favour, so you muster up a little courage. Then you hear a voice that's not in your favour, and you are slimed again. You carry so many bags of false guilt that you are stooped over.

You allow yourself a crumb; eating the entire piece of pie is for others. You keep yourself in your place by "crumb-eating." You keep yourself dutiful and responsible and you avoid taking chances because you fear making a mistake. You're a good person and good people don't make waves or even ripples. You don't rock the boat and upset anyone else; you *fear* that—you'd rather die than do that! By nature, you do not think about your own well-being. You keep the peace at all costs, including yours.

Your antenna is up, scouting the land and picking up signals. Excessive guilt lets your mind wander down a path of no return. *What if I've done the wrong thing?* you wonder frantically. *How will this affect everyone else? What are the ramifications? What are the consequences? How will I endure disapproval? Will someone abandon me? Will someone say something bad about me?*

Your mind is filled with self-doubt and you think you will never get out of this "episode" of guilt. Everything that you intend to do shuts down. The faucet of freedom is off.

My friend, guilt is depression talking to you! Lift your head and look up at Jesus. He died for you and *that's* why he intercedes for you. His face has a smile, not a frown, upon your life. *You are worth what you need.* Don't ever forget that.

Action Step

When does guilt bring you anguish? Bring it into the light. Discuss it with a trusted friend. Try to identify false guilt. Take in the validation of others and God. Write "You are worth what you need" and put it on your bathroom mirror. Read it daily, and when the guilt floods in, answer back, "I am worth what I need."

Prayer

Lord, who can condemn me? No one, according to Your Word, because You died for my sin and guilt. It's a lie that I'm guilty and have to feel that way all the time. It's a spiritual battle. You are for me, not against me. So when those lies invade my mind, help me to confront them with truth that the God of this universe is on my side.

My Journal

The New Normal

Scripture

"In the same way the Spirit also helps our weakness; for we do not know how to pray as we should, but the Spirit Himself intercedes for us with groanings too deep for words; and He who searches the hearts knows what the mind of the Spirit is, because He intercedes for the saints according to the will of God. And we know that God causes all things to work together for good to those who love God, to those who are called according to His purpose." ROMANS 8:26-28 (NASB)

"Job continued speaking: 'I long for the years gone by when God took care of me, when he lit up the way before me and I walked safely through the darkness.'" JOB 29:1-3 (NLT)

"And now my life seeps away. Depression haunts my days." JOB 30:16 (NLT)

Message

I dusted Romans 8:28 off of the shelf recently and read it as though I had never read that verse before, and it confounded me. My thinking had been so off-track that I'd felt as though I was out of God's reach. I had been so blinded by my circumstances that I couldn't see him; I had lost sight of him completely.

Grieving involves setting aside time to acknowledge our thoughts and feelings with the goal of accepting the "new normal." My mother died in February and the aftershocks came in waves at the most unexpected times. The grieving was not so much about what actually *was*, but what *could have been*. A lot of our grieving is about what could have been, or what we thought *should* have been. The "new normal" is never what we expect; that's part of the deep grieving process. Setting aside time to acknowledge our thoughts and feelings regarding our "new normal" is a very crucial and meditative step in our healing.

You may feel completely unprepared to deal with this now. But in an effort to promote healing, I challenge you to consider the following questions. What are the events you did not expect to come your way? What did you think would happen instead? How do you feel about the transitions in your life? What hopes for someone did you have that did not materialize and how has that affected your life? How sad are you about a particular outcome? Do you fear your future, and why? Has something happened to you that you don't understand? Are you extremely worried about someone or something? What have you not come to terms with?

The mind has a way of constantly trying to "fix" things. When it can't, the emotions become imbedded in our souls. We continue acquiring layer upon layer of loss. It is like looking at the layers below the earth's surface. If we can barrel down through each layer, the crust, the mantel, and the outer core, we eventually get to the inner core. We can't begin the healing process until we dig deep into the inner core of our issues.

We have to look back so we can look forward. We have to look reality dead in the face and acknowledge what is. We need to come to a place of acceptance so we can embrace our "new normal." Although it may be difficult, it is possible to accept our "new normal." If we refuse, we will cling to dreams that never materialize. Despite our lives taking some unexpected detours, we can still live fulfilling and purposeful lives. We can create new and different hopes and dreams; some may be even more wonderful than we could have ever imagined. We must be gentle with ourselves during this transition. We can forgive ourselves and others on our journey to our "new normal." We can—and must—start from where we are.

In Carol Kent's books *When I Lay My Isaac Down* and *The New Normal,* she explains how life-altering events—events that change us forever—create our "new normal." These events can be illness, financial loss, divorce, relational splits, physical abuse, emotional abuse, sexual abuse, death, childhood pain, mental illness, unplanned pregnancy, or any unexpected tragedy.

Action Step

Set aside time to acknowledge your thoughts and feelings with the goal of accepting the "new normal." Put on paper what was and what is. What life-altering experiences have you come to know? How can you start life with a new definition? How can you embrace these events, learning from them what you might otherwise never know?

Prayer

Lord, the giant surprises of life make me gasp at times. I did not expect this outcome and I may not want this outcome. Things can happen suddenly. I find transitions and changes hard to deal with. I have to adjust to change and I know that through Your strength, I am able to adjust. I appeal to Your sovereignty over my life and ask You to help me trust in You when the unthinkable happens.

My Journal

My Journal

DAY THIRTY

The Lowest Stave

Scripture

"For it is better, if God should will it so, that you suffer for doing what is right rather than for doing what is wrong."
I PETER 3:17 (NASB)

"But no one puts a patch of unshrunk cloth on an old garment; for the patch pulls away from the garment, and a worse tear results. Nor do people put new wine into old wineskins; otherwise the wineskins burst, and the wine pours out and the wineskins are ruined; but they put new wine into fresh wineskins, and both are preserved." MATTHEW 9:16-17 (NASB)

"Therefore, confess your sins to one another, and pray for one another so that you may be healed. The effective prayer of a righteous man can accomplish much." JAMES 5:16 (NASB)

Meditation

In Christian Schwarz's book, *Natural Church Development,* he presents his studies of 1,000 churches in 32 countries; through these studies, he discovered eight essentials that, without fail, are always true of growing churches. One of those essentials is "functional structures." Dr. Schwarz explains "functional structures" as practices that exist only to help the church fulfill its stated purpose for existence. If a structure does not accomplish its purpose, it is considered "nonfunctional" and must be eliminated. The goal is to develop structures that undergird the process of healthy development for any given church.

The same principles apply in our lives. We need functional structures that undergird our particular process of growth, addressing our specific needs and foibles resulting from depression and anxiety. If the structures do not accomplish the goals we want to achieve, we must reassess our structures. Sometimes, our lives need a radical realignment with the proper priorities being placed at the top of the list.

As I discussed in "Bucket Friends" (day nineteen), a bucket can only hold water to the height of its lowest stave. Maybe water—anxiety and depression—is pouring out of our buckets, our lives, due to dysfunctional staves, the coping mechanisms we use to deal with our anxiety and depression.

We may feel a great deal of fear addressing the real issues, but ultimately we will be healthier and become whole if we do address our issues. We will want to tackle the barricades that block our recovery and devise healthier plans and options. We will want to reassess our journey and examine what brought us to the place of such profound depression. I don't know your stressors and I don't know your provision, but I know that God does.

I want to address the lowest stave analogy by talking about our pain and embracing it in healthier ways. Learning to focus on the possible benefits of pain may shed new light on living with an eternal mindset.

There are different kinds of pain. Sometimes our pain is self-inflicted, other times we suffer because we did the "right thing," and other times we are simply a victim of an imperfect world filled with pain and disease. This world is still under the fall, and it may, at times, fall on us.

I maintain that the church often inflicts pain instead of providing healing. Those of us suffering from anxiety and depression already feel anxious about our struggles. We are often told to read Scripture and pray harder, but our attempts to do so may not reduce our pain but only heap on more guilt and shame. What we need is a safe place—an "environmental hospital"—free of judgment and full of safety and support for us to express our truth. We need authenticity and validation from church leadership and we need to know we are not alone.

As an annual holiday was approaching, I attended a local church service. The pastor raved about his "perfect" family with adult children who all married Christ followers. He attributed this wonderful scenario to the blessings of God. It may have been true, but I knew he had lost upward of 60% of his congregation who wished such were true of their own lives.

We don't want to reinjure others who are already wounded. Below are examples of using healing words versus re-wounding words in our interactions with those who are suffering. The following was written by a therapist friend, Dawn Angelich (MFT):

A parent who has lost a child in death
Healing touch:

"I'm here in any way you might need."

"Anytime you want to talk about your child, I want to share with you in your memories."

Wounding touch:

"At least you know your child is with Jesus."

"Time will heal."

"At least you were blessed to have those years with your child."

"Just look what God has done as a result of your child's death."

A person with a chronic/terminal illness
Healing touch:

"I would like to help you in a practical way. Can I come over to bring a meal? Do the laundry? Pick up prescriptions? Do some errands?"

"What would be a good time for me to call you and get mini updates on how I could specifically pray for your needs?"

Wounding touch:

"Just let me know if you need anything." *(A sick person doesn't have the energy to initiate asking for what they need!)*

"Know that I will be praying for you." *(But then never calling again to see how the sick person is doing.)*

A person with marital struggles
Healing touch:

"No matter how your relationship ends up, know that I am your friend and I care about you."

Possibly recommend pastoral and/or professional counselling as a resource for additional support.

Wounding touch:

Pry or give advice as to what *you think* the person should or shouldn't do. This fosters a parent-child kind of friendship instead of an adult-to-adult friendship.

Action Step

Take some time to think through practical and helpful ways you may bring a measure of healing to someone. Consider the suggestions above. Identify a place of personal wounding. Persist in learning healing behaviours and ways of living with yourself and others.

Prayer

Lord, I'm the harshest critic of myself. Why is that? I'm not nice to myself. But You give me value and meaning. I can come up with no other conclusion. I have had painful things happen to me. I have wounds that need to heal. Heal me, Lord. Fix what is broken in my heart. I ask You, dear Lord, to show me the ways in which I can be kind to myself.

My Journal

The Wounded Healer

Scripture

"Therefore, strengthen the hands that are weak and the knees that are feeble, and make straight paths for your feet, so that the limb that is lame may not be put out of joint, but rather be healed." HEBREWS 12:12-13 (NASB)

"And hearing this, Jesus said to them, 'It is not those who are healthy who need a physician, but those who are sick; I did not come to call the righteous, but sinners.'" MARK 2:17 (NASB)

Meditation

Recently, the battery in my red car malfunctioned. The car and I had to be towed to the dealership. The tow-truck driver was mystified as to why he couldn't get my car to respond to an infusion from the jumper cables since the car was under warranty and low in mileage. Nothing made sense, so the only option was for us to go for a ride on the freeway with the car in tow. We were in the slow lane, high above the whizzing traffic below us, and we had time to talk.

I told him that my dryer had broken down that morning, too. He looked at me with all the wisdom of a "master of distress" and said, "Breakdowns come in threes." Little did I know that the third breakdown of the day would be me!

I have been stopped dead in my tracks. Just as my car would not respond to jumper cables, my heart and soul have been unable to respond to my world. The battery of my life has not been functioning. I have found myself in a season of emotional debilitation. However, this may change. A year from now, I may read my own writings and they may seem foreign to me, as though I won't recognize the person who wrote them.

Broken people are all around us. They are sitting next to us in the pews or folding chairs at church. They live in our neighbourhoods and in our complexes. They work in our offices. They visit and live in our homes. They sit in our book clubs and small groups. But we may never know about these broken souls. They are desperate for help, but they don't know who to ask, who to tell, or how to find it. They feel hopeless, as if they have no options.

St. Francis of Assisi said, "We are called to heal wounds, to unite what has fallen apart, and to bring home those who have lost their way." This should be the mission statement of the church. If my journey of pain had a voice, it would be this message to the church, the body of Christ: The church needs to be a place of refuge!

Sometimes, we do not identify the church as a friend. We may notice congregations divided into cliques; the die has been cast and the groups are impenetrable. Their history does not include us. We may have reached out and been rebuked. The body of Christ is imperfect; the addition of mortal humans made it that way. I loved serving the church, and I still believe in it because Jesus is perfecting it. *We* are the church!

My husband and I recently attended a church service, and it was a beautiful experience of revelation for me. The congregation is usually sparse, but for some reason, the church was packed. The pastor spoke from Matthew 9:27-31, about Jesus' healing of two men who were blind. In a very authentic, well-delivered message about healing, the congregation was invited to come forward and receive prayer and anointing with oil by elders. I had not gone forward in church since childhood, but I believe I was led by the Holy Spirit to accept the invitation to the altar. When my husband turned around, he realized I was one with the mass of people moving toward the front of the church. I keenly observed the large number of folks who looked so "perfect" on the outside, but stood humbly in line for prayer, just like me. The warm hands of the couple who prayed over me represented the warmth of God's love.

William P. Young, author of *The Shack*, has done a mystifying work of giving us a glimpse of God's heart. The author's personal story bears the pain of which he writes. The religious righteous brought injury to him as a young child, and the abuse evidenced itself in his adult years. He writes about his disillusionment with the church. He proposed that if the church functioned as it was meant to function, there would be little need for so many "professional healers." Sadly, the church often reinjures people. However, you should not give up on the church. If you do not contribute, someone very important is missing. You need to seek out safe places where you can minister and be ministered to.

I pray for you during your time of anguish and pain. I trust you will seek healing. May God have mercy on you. You are not alone.

Action Step

How can you reach out in grace? How can you contribute to authenticity? How can your anxiety and depression be an avenue of safety for another sufferer? The church is missing something when you are not contributing. What is *real* church for you? Who is community? How do you seek to build Christian community? Really think about your answers to these questions.

Prayer

Lord, You came for the sick and not those who are well. You said so. Many people feel as though they have to be well before they come to You. I'm not well, and neither are they. Help me to find those who feel on the fringes and need words of love. Show me Your love today. Help me to show Your love to others.

My Journal

My Journal

Distraction

Scripture

"Therefore, humble yourselves under the mighty hand of God, that He may exalt you at the proper time, casting all your anxiety on Him, because He cares for you." I PETER 5:6-7 (NASB)

"Because of the surpassing greatness of the revelations, for this reason, to keep me from exalting myself, there was given to me a thorn in the flesh, a messenger of Satan to torment me, to keep me from exalting myself! Concerning this, I implored the Lord three times that it might leave me. And He said to me, 'My grace is sufficient for you, for power is perfected in weakness.' Most gladly, therefore, I will rather boast about my weaknesses, so that the power of Christ may dwell in me. Therefore, I am well content with weaknesses, with insults, with distresses, with persecutions, with difficulties, for Christ's sake; for when I am weak, then I am strong."
II CORINTHIANS 12:7-10 (NASB)

Meditation

No one has ruled out the possibility that the Apostle Paul may have suffered from an anxiety disorder or severe depression. Paul simply did not disclose his suffering, leaving the option wide open.

Depression has been, and continues to be, a reality in my life. Its progression plays out for me as follows. A precipitator triggers bad feelings—it could be a glance, an angry word, an unreturned phone call or e-mail, something that triggers past trauma, or disorientation. Then, the bad feelings evolve into shame or guilt, which leads to self-loathing and progresses to a deep sense of worthlessness and feelings of stupidity.

Recently, a minister shared with me that two years prior, he fell into a deep, depressive "funk" that he was unable to escape. The depression became painfully debilitating. Anxiety would hit and he would become extremely irritable. In this irritable state, he said hurtful things and behaved in ways he later regretted. Then the self-loathing set in, resulting in depression.

He took his first step toward recovery by seeing a therapist. He was diagnosed with dysthymia, a type of chronic, low-grade depression. Upon his diagnosis, his therapist referred him to a psychiatrist. The psychiatrist prescribed a 15-mg selective serotonin reuptake inhibitor, an antidepressant that restored his outlook on life within two days. If he takes his medication and fish oil and maintains his regular exercise, he manages life very well. Overcoming the stigma of taking medication for a mental condition was the most difficult part of his depressive episode. But good friends reasoned with him. If he had diabetes, would he not take insulin? If he had high blood pressure, would he not take medication? Taking the proper medication for mental ailments is no less important than it is for physical ailments. We need not be ashamed.

Like the minister, my progression continues on the depression continuum. I experience giant leaps of despair into distorted thinking. My depression also manifests itself as dreadful anxiety and mortal terror.

The last leap into the quicksand involves catastrophic feelings and deep fears of being permanently debilitated by the depression. In an attempt to allay the anxiety, I try to find my way inside the eye of the hurricane and untwist the twister. This anxiety-fighting technique of distraction takes no less wit or force to employ than the twister of emotions takes.

While inside the eye of the hurricane, I debilitate the gale by reminding myself that I only need to hold on for *just one more day.* Then I know that distraction is okay. Distractions are activities or choices we can make that are stronger than the pull of the anxiety. They are not only okay, but also crucial in disabling anxiety and moving toward healing. I choose to place my anxiety at the feet of the Lord and engage in another activity. I put one foot in front of the other, whether I want to or not. If I choose distraction, it's like pulling an electric cord out of a socket—the electrical pulse of anxiety stops, if only for a moment.

As part of my daily self-care, I recite the prayer of Reinhold Niebuhr: "God grant me the serenity to accept the things I cannot change; courage to change the things I can; and wisdom to know the difference. This means living one day at a time, enjoying one moment at a time, accepting hardships as the pathway to peace, and taking as he did this sinful world as it is, not as I would have it." This means "trusting that he will make all things right if I surrender to his will; that

I may be reasonably happy in this life and supremely happy with him forever in the next." *(see appendix called "In My Control.")*

When we find ourselves in the midst of anxiety, it is probably too difficult to think creatively about diversions. Today's action step encourages us to choose preemptive strategies before anxiety gets a gravitational pull on us.

Action Step

Think of five possible distractions you can choose to "trick" anxiety. What strongly engages your interest enough to conquer anxiety? Choose these activities as necessary.

1. _____
2. _____
3. _____
4. _____
5. _____

Prayer

Lord, I can cast all my cares on You with a big "heave-ho." I can throw them on Your back. What a relief! There are things for which You do not provide relief, yet You provide grace. Things hurt; I sometimes feel like I'm walking on gravel without shoes on. You do not always remove my infirmities, but those hurts can help me to depend on You for everything. Lord, I depend on You to help me.

My Journal

Fantasy and Reality

Scripture

"Not that I speak from want, for I have learned to be content in whatever circumstances I am. I know how to get along with humble means, and I also know how to live in prosperity; in any and every circumstance I have learned the secret of being filled and going hungry, both of having abundance and suffering need. I can do all things through Him who strengthens me." PHILIPPIANS 4:11-13 (NASB)

"And when I was present with you and was in need, I was not a burden to anyone; for when the brethren came from Macedonia, they fully supplied my need, and in everything I kept myself from being a burden to you, and will continue to do so." II CORINTHIANS 11:9 (NASB)

"For I am not ashamed of the gospel, for it is the power of God for salvation to everyone who believes."
ROMANS 1:16A, B (NASB)

Meditation

A businessperson once said that 80% of the people in the workforce are not in a perfect job match. When is the last time we heard someone say, "I love what I do"? A woman told me that she wishes everyone had the privilege in life to love what he or she does for a living. This has been her unique experience. She found her job through an unexpected connection and she discovered her gifts and talents perfectly suited her nine-to-five job.

In the book *Love It Don't Leave It,* the authors state that the average person spends a full 17 years, or almost 149,000 hours, of his or her life working. Seventeen years is a lot of time to do something we do not enjoy. Life is short; how we spend the time we are given is precious.

"I love what I do" has been a painful statement for me to hear because I've been searching for a way to be paid for what I love to do. I have felt that my anxiety has been a hindrance in that pursuit.

Ideally, we would all find ourselves living out our passions vocationally. If we put the need for money aside, what could or would we see ourselves doing? Our passions and our careers are not necessarily mutually exclusive. The Apostle Paul lived on the gifts of others as well as being a tentmaker. He loved sharing the gospel more than anything else. In fact, he shared the gospel while he was chained in jail (Acts 16) while tentmaking, or travelling, all with fabulous results. His circumstances did not hinder his passion. He found a way to incorporate it into his life, regardless of what he was doing.

I faced a dilemma while attending seminary, working toward my master's degree. I was also working in a ministry position and was busy as the mother of a young child. The demands of motherhood, taking care of a home, working, and studying took a heavy toll on my family and me; something had to give. I sought counsel and received mixed reviews. Ultimately, I let go of my seminary studies and focused on parenting. It was a tough decision, but facing reality meant that I could not do everything I wanted.

However, this decision did not mean I had to stop learning altogether. I have been able to acquire certification and continue academic pursuits where tuition has been involved. I still pursued higher education, but in a different vein. This has been a way to recover some of the loss of not obtaining my master's.

We need to learn to be both realistic and to strive to meet our unmet needs, goals, and desires in the way we live our lives. The best way to accomplish this is through compromise or reprioritization. If we put health and well-being first, then we may live with less, requiring less income. Sometimes, like the Apostle Paul, we use our job to attend to the basics of salary and benefits, but we can also look for opportunities to incorporate our gifts and talents into our job descriptions.

Eric Liddell, the British track athlete who competed in the 1924 Paris Summer Olympics, said, "When I run, I feel God's pleasure." He was known as the athlete who ran for God. Liddell competed in the Olympic Games but eventually returned to the call of missions, his truest passion. Because of Liddell's religious faith, he was imprisoned in 1943 in a concentration camp in Weishan, China, where he eventually and unfortunately died.

As a vocational minister, I was amazed at how little I was taught about preparing for my aging years. I was told that if I trusted God, he would take care of it all. The fallacy was not about God; it was about the reality of us living far beyond our prime earning years. I was definitely living out my passion in vocational ministry during my 20s, but during my 50s, I experienced a monetary cost for which no one prepared me.

Although most of us would love to pursue our passions and dreams, we must marry fantasy and reality. If we put our passions and dreams on the backburner for too long, they may never be realized. We don't want to feel as if everything is on the top shelf, out of our reach. However, living our passions must include planning for the future financially. It is imperative to plan wisely yet allow some margin to enjoy life without feeling too deprived.

Many people are able to engage in both work and passion. If it all possible, we should strive to align our work to follow our passion. However, we may have seasons in our lives that govern our pursuits. We may not want to do what we are currently doing for the long term, but it may be necessary to carry on longer than planned. Our passions, like Paul's tentmaking, and our means of provision are not necessarily mutually exclusive.

Action Step

Every one of us has a "pleasure zone." We experience this zone when we are fully engrossed in using the best of our gifts and talents. We usually feel energized and lose all track of time. Ask yourself when it is that you feel God's pleasure. Dream the dream. Seek it!

Prayer

*Lord, there is a big difference between fantasy
and reality. I need to face reality in a brutal
way and confront the truest things about
myself and about life. I also have dreams and
hopes that You care about. Your thoughts about
me outnumber my own. Lord, You create
the desires of my heart; provide me a way to
achieve something I'd very much like to do.*

My Journal

Provision

Scripture

"Isaac spoke to Abraham his father and said, 'My father.' And he said, 'Here I am, my son.' And he said, 'Behold, the fire and the wood, but where is the lamb for the burnt offering?' Abraham said, 'God will provide for Himself the lamb for the burnt offering, my son.' So the two of them walked on together. Abraham called the name of that place The Lord Will Provide, as it is said to this day, 'In the mount of the Lord it will be provided.'" GENESIS 22: 7-8, 14 (NASB)

Meditation

In the Bible verses above, Abraham obeyed God without hesitation, although he had not always done so. Earlier in his life, he lied about his wife's identity in order to protect his backside. He also collaborated with Sarah to borrow her handmaiden to conceive Ishmael. Abraham was not always God's "you-can-count-on-him-guy."

However, Abraham's trust of God grew, and he walked the Mount with Isaac on this occasion without question. Abraham had been through enough to trust God's provision. There had been such horrible fall-out whenever he'd doubted, that he didn't think twice. (We will leave to speculation the perceptions of Isaac lying under a lifted knife.)

If this journey of anxiety and depression had a companion, it would be, "How will God provide?" Draining 401Ks and living lean has not been my idea of anxiety resolution.

Recently, I was walking through the market when a woman with an apron came from the yogourt-sampling exhibit in the dairy section, running swiftly past me. Our paths crossed exactly at the same point in the produce section when she exclaimed, "This is a miracle!" Without being obnoxious, I was bold enough to ask her about her excitement.

She stopped and said, "I have to tell someone." I told her I was all ears and she happily and enthusiastically obliged. She had moved from another state, foreclosed on a home, and left family behind to relocate in California. She spent some time homeless and was currently renting a room in a nearby city. In addition to distributing samples for various companies, she worked as a mystery shopper.

One of her assignments was to visit a local car dealership, where she was supposed to evaluate the salespeople and their customer service. She had to act like a regular customer, asking all the typical questions about the various car brands, features, prices, and financing. Because mystery shoppers are anonymous, the salesperson thought she was interested in buying a car. After all her probing questions, why would he think otherwise? He implored her to think about buying a new car. She scoffed—she knew she was in no position to purchase a car because her credit scores had tanked.

Besides, she wasn't there to buy a car; she was there on assignment. However, the salesman persisted.

I would presume, out of charity and the need to sell a car, the salesman suggested she leave her car—which was clearly dated and rundown—as collateral and try out one of nice loaner cars for the day to see how she liked it. Just before we bumped into each other at the market, she'd received a call on her cell phone, informing her that the car she had on loan was hers for the right price; apparently, the salesman worked out a deal that fit into her budget. All he needed was a signature to close the deal.

The woman told me her name was Beverly (my name)! In the course of our conversation, she said, "God will provide" more than five times. She also told me she was a believing Christian who was trying to pull her life together by reconnecting with God. She said this miracle was a definite tug in the right direction. She knew she had unfinished business, but she was already taking care of that. She and her pastor had prayed together the night before about putting her life back together.

She told me she liked me and that I, too, could trust God for provision. Was this an angel? Angel or not, I took to heart what she said about trusting God for provision.

There is a story that has appeared and reappeared in many sermons about God's provision. It is meant as a joke, but there is truth behind it. It goes something like this: There is a flood and a man crawls on his roof to avoid peril. God sends a rowboat along and a man asks if he can help. The man on the roof says, "No, thanks"—he has prayed and God is going to take care of him. So God sends a rescue helicopter but the man on the roof has the same response. The third effort on God's part is met with the same reaction. Then, the man drowns and goes to heaven, where he asks God why he did not rescue him. God told him that he tried, three different times, but was turned down!

Although it may look different from what we expect, we need to be open to God's provision. We may not see God's provision through the trees of the forest. Maybe it isn't our idea of provision, or our pride may stand in the way. We might have to ask for help; God will not ask for us. Maybe the right people need to know we need help. Maybe provision is a different kind of bow on the package, and the gift is thrown out along with the bow.

I am grateful for how provision has come into my life. I never thought state disability would be a way of provision. Although it's humiliating, I'm thankful. A friend of mine, who is my size, has clothes to spare. I've benefited from additional articles of clothing during a time when I could not afford to purchase any. I have received many forms of help, such as emotional support from friends, food, counsel with a wise therapist, friends, several gifted massages, and an unexpected gift of cash at Christmas from a family member.

Action Step

For whom have you observed God providing? How has He provided for you in small ways and big ways? What do you languish over regarding provision at this time? Do you need to pray and tell someone? Review your gratefulness journal and see what you have. If you haven't started one yet, put on your thinking cap and come up with all the provisions God has granted you. You can make your own "count your blessings" list.

Prayer

Lord, I always feel like it's all up to me; that I'm on my own and I have to do everything. Why is that? I've had to make too many things happen on my own. But I know that You provide in ways I do not see. Help me to trust You more.

My Journal

The Ship's Rudder

Scripture

"They passed through the Phrygian and Galatian region, having been forbidden by the Holy Spirit to speak the word in Asia; and after they came to Mysia, they were trying to go into Bithynia, and the Spirit of Jesus did not permit them; and passing by Mysia, they came down to Troas. A vision appeared to Paul in the night: a certain man of Macedonia was standing and appealing to him, and saying, 'Come over to Macedonia and help us.'"
ACTS 16:6-9 (NASB)

Meditation

During the writing of this book, my anxiety is the worst first thing in the morning. I have such difficulty gripping on to a meditation. That is why I've written this—for those who may have trouble in the morning hours to be drawn into quiet time with God. I often have to pick other times of the day when I can focus and concentrate.

Recently, in the midst of my anxiety, I picked up my well-worn copy of the devotional book, *Streams in the Desert*. It was my father's copy and bears my orange colouring in the front inside flap from when I was a toddler. The words from the September 24 entry settled me.

In Acts 16:6-9, notice that Paul was having difficulty arriving at the right place at the right time; God was saying "no." A hallmark of my prolonged period of anxiety and depression has been the apparent absence of direction. For example, I'm now infamous for being a "professional interviewee." I have walked through many a door, only to have it slammed in my face. I have had tears and days of confusion. For some reason, God was closing doors, saying "no."

One memory is stark. I had applied for a position that replicated my duties in my former company. The company's VP had narrowed down the pile of resumes to just two—and one of them was mine. The VP and I had a number of interactions. The position opened at the right time and I would have taken it. The same week, however, the company relocated the position to another state; my job search halted once again.

Slowly and painfully, God has been shedding everything necessary to prepare me for the next season. God has been narrowing my focus.

The September 24 entry in *Streams in the Desert* reads: "What a strange prohibition! These men were going to Bithynia just to do Christ's work, and the door is shut against them by Christ's own Spirit. I, too, have experienced this in certain moments. I have sometimes found myself interrupted in what seemed to me a career of usefulness. Opposition came and forced me to go back, or sickness came and compelled me to retire into a desert apart. And so, Thou Divine Spirit, would I still be led by Thee. Still there came to me disappointed prospects of usefulness. Today the door seems to open into life and work for Thee; tomorrow it closes before me just as I am about to enter. Teach me to see another door in the very inaction of the hour" (written by George Matheson).

Matheson came to learn that the "desert place apart is often the most useful spot in the varied life of man—more rich in harvest than the seasons in which the corn and wine abound."

Even when God is closing doors or saying "no," we need to keep moving. A rudder for a moving ship is not only useful, but also necessary. But the rudder is rendered useless for a ship that is docked. In Acts, we see that Paul moved, but it was the Spirit who led. We, too, need to keep moving and let the Spirit guide.

Action Step

Keep moving in spite of the confusion. Each step is an opportunity for the rudder of your ship to guide you. Try not to devalue yourself and succumb to inaction in the midst of redirection. Instead, let the redirection thrust you forward on to the next opportunity.

Prayer

Lord, I need Your guidance. Life feels so meaningless at times and my efforts so futile. I have to try. I have to walk through doors or into them while You close them and open others. My part is to keep walking. A ship's rudder is only useful to a moving ship. I want to move and find that You have led me in the way I need to go. With You at my side, help me to stay on the right path that leads to righteousness.

My Journal

Threat Appraisal

Scripture

"Trust in the Lord with all your heart, and do not lean on your own understanding. In all your ways acknowledge Him, and He will make your paths straight." PROVERBS 3: 5-6 (NASB)

Meditation

Living with anxiety is like living with a broken compass. As I've mentioned before, anxiety does not lead us due north. Our journey often reveals that anxiety is leading *us*, instead of the other way around. A spiritual mentor of more than 20 years pointed this out to me. He said that we can make a decision and *still* experience anxiety. We follow the anxiety and make another decision based on our anxiety, and so it continues. While stuck in this pattern, our anxiety drives our choices. Cognitive therapy can help us because it deals with our thought distortions and trains our minds to trump our feelings. This, in turn, activates our compass in the proper direction: north.

Self-doubt is one of my mortal wounds. I've been rehearsing and regurgitating angles on various decisions I have made. Second-guessing becomes a source of anxiety and my mind begins to obsess repeatedly on the same issue. This is true of those who struggle with anxiety—we obsess over perceived threats. Our threat appraisal is distorted, however; our sense of "normal" is bent out of shape. It's analogous to an eating disorder in this way: Sufferers lose a sense of what is normal in their desire for food and their feeling of being satiated. So it is with those of us who suffer from anxiety; our adrenalin continues to pump, even in the absence of threat. We have trouble differentiating between real and imagined threats. We lump everything together and feel preoccupied with danger where none exists.

Dr. Jill Bolte, a brain scientist and author of *A Stroke of Insight*, shares some insights about the brain. "When incoming stimulation is perceived as familiar, the amygdale (a key component of the brain, involved in the experience of anxiety) is calm and the adjacently positioned hippocampus (the part of the brain that controls memory) is capable of learning and memorizing new information. However, as soon as the amygdale is triggered by unfamiliar or perhaps threatening stimulation, it raises the brain's level of anxiety and focuses the mind's attention on the immediate situation. Under these circumstances, our attention is shifted away from the hippocampus and focused toward self-preserving behaviour about the present moment."

The brain goes into a "fight or flight" mode, which is essential under drastic circumstances. But if this mode is maintained for long periods without a present threat, it can actually rewire neurotransmitters in the brain.

We do not have to be anxious when there is no threat present. We have to let go of our obsessions of perceived threats. We have to learn to determine when our vigilance is needed and when it is not. We can do this by thinking things through and attending to a more realistic perspective. We can choose to avoid giving our words and thoughts more power than they truly have. We can ask God to help us think clearly and rationally and to give us peace of mind. When God is part of our equation, we do not have to be unnecessarily anxious.

Action Step

Take a look at the document at the back of the book called "In My Control." Use it to discern what you are able to control and what you are not. See if it aids your process in threat assessment.

Prayer

Lord, sometimes I live like there is a burglar at my door and I know it is anxiety. I become scared when there is nothing to fear. There is so much over which I have no control. Help me to save my energy for when I really need it. I do not want to live a co-dependent life, but I will need Your help with this. The feeling of threat can be real. Help me not to live in a "fear mode". I ask that You wrap a blanket of peace and contentment over me.

My Journal

The Thorn in the Flesh

Scripture

"For even when we came into Macedonia our flesh had no rest, but we were afflicted on every side: conflicts without, fears within. But God, who comforts the depressed, comforted us by the coming of Titus; and not only by his coming, but also by the comfort with which he was comforted in you, as he reported to us your longing, your mourning, your zeal for me; so that I rejoiced even more." II CORINTHIANS 7:5-7 (NASB)

Meditation

I want to make a case for the possibility that Paul's thorn from the above Scripture passage was clinical depression.

1. Paul experienced affliction and conflicts "without" (outward circumstances) and fears "within" (the internal anxiety) (v. 5)
2. In the next breath, Paul references "the depressed," which likely referred to him, according to the context (v. 6)
3. God comforts the depressed (v. 6)
4. He uses other people (Titus) to do the comforting (v. 6)
5. Titus comforted simply through his presence ("by his coming") (v. 7)

6. Part of the comfort for Paul was Titus' report about how much he was valued by the others back in Corinth (v. 7)

Throughout church history, various phrases have been used to describe depression, such as "disease of melancholy." This is not a new condition. C. H. Spurgeon, born in 1834 in England, was known as the "Prince of Preachers." He died in 1892 and by the time of his death, he had preached 3,600 sermons. His audiences often numbered more than 10,000 people. However, he apparently had struggled with clinical depression for many years and spoke of being moved to tears for no reason known to him.

The truth I want to identify is the way in which God comforted Paul. He sent a real live person through the presence of Titus. God did not ask Paul to pray and read his Bible more; he knew Paul needed flesh-and-bones help. It is such comfort to sit with a comforter; it's like pulling up a blanket in the cold. Titus was that blanket for Paul.

It is also encouraging to hear how we have touched a life, just as Paul needed to hear. Even in the midst of our pain, we can still minister to others. I had the pleasure of attending a fundraiser at a church where I once worked. I was greeted with a plethora of hugs and squeezes. My soul took courage in knowing my life had influenced these people, even to this day. Even though I suffered periods of anxiety and depression, it did not diminish my ministry.

Do not believe the lie that we cannot minister while experiencing pain. Often, pain is the pathway of ministry.

Action Step

Make a list of lives you have touched for the good; these are the jewels in your crown. Do not underestimate your ability to reach out, despite both mental and physical pain.

Prayer

Lord, even the Apostle Paul was depressed. So many leaders of Your church have been depressed. It is not a sign of sin or weakness. Help me to embrace my anxiety and depression for the unexpected strength that comes as a result.

My Journal

Emotional De-Cluttering

Scripture

"Therefore, strengthen the hands that are weak and the knees that are feeble, and make straight paths for your feet, so that the limb that is lame may not be put out of joint, but rather be healed." HEBREWS 12: 12-13 (NASB)

Meditation

In Greek, the word "healed" refers to spiritual healing; the word "sin" refers to missing the mark, falling short, and the governing power that works against the body of Christ. In Hebrews 12:12-13, Paul is writing in the context of those who observe our faith. With this in mind, we must be very careful to lay aside every encumbrance, weight, and sin that besets us, so we can fix our eyes on Jesus, who will ultimately perfect our faith.

What encumbrances, weights, flaws, wounds, losses, weaknesses, distresses, persecutions, difficulties, suffering, angst, and sins beset us?

It has been proven that the endorphins in our brain increase when we de-clutter our environment. The endorphins are the "good stuff" in our brains—the stuff that increases when we exercise and laugh. A lot of us need to emotionally de-clutter, as well. We all have losses and wounds that plague us. It may not be the big swords, but rather the little gnats that keep flying around our brain, that bug us. If we were asked to identify our emotional gnats, what would they be? One example might be a man who has always wanted to marry. He walks behind a couple holding hands, and feels pain. It reminds him that life has turned out differently than he had expected.

Pearls are timeless. Jackie Onassis wore them and women still wear them today. Pearls are created from irritation, harvested off the blue marine shores of Hawaii. A natural pearl begins its life as a foreign object, such as a parasite of shell that accidentally lodges itself in an oyster's soft inner body, where it cannot be expelled. To ease this irritant, the oyster's body takes defensive action. The oyster begins to secrete a smooth, hard crystalline substance around the irritant in order to protect itself. This process brings us the precious pearl.

I was sitting in a job interview, wearing a pair of mother of pearl hoop earrings that I'd bought in Ko Olina, Hawaii. During my interview, an individual gave me a startling compliment. He said he believed my life was like my pearl earrings—that beauty would result from the irritants in my life. It was highly unusual that he had such insight because I shared no "personal irritants" with him. But those beautiful words are still lodged in my mind, just like the irritant in the oyster that produces the beautiful pearl.

I believe it is biblical for our irritants to become the pearls that grace our lives; they represent feats of redemption. But how do we allow our irritants to become pearls? Is there a well-worn path that no one has told us about? Is there a forged place in the forest of life that we haven't found? Is it an easy road or is it the narrow way?

When I was in Hawaii, I hiked the rain forest north of Honolulu and I was struck with the Amazon green beauty, the gnarled branches of trees, and the fern grottos larger than life. The path was slippery and muddy and the hike, winding and hard, but getting to the top to see the waterfall was worth the arduous journey. Suffering through the irritants in our lives is what brings us to the beauty.

Action Step

Take a step toward recovery by acknowledging the emotional gnats in your life that represent the loss. Clear up your heart by bringing them to God. Ask Him to turn them into feats of redemption.

Prayer

Lord, there are irritants in my life that I experience as boils on my skin. Loss, mistakes, self-deception, awful feelings, worries, wrong choices, and much more. You are the only one who majors in redemption. It's Your offer to the world and to me. You can take what I break and fix it; through the repairs, it will become even more beautiful. You create out of my garbage can. You love to make my life beautiful. I invite You to continue doing so.

My Journal

DAY THIRTY-NINE

Working with What We Have

Scripture

"For thus says the Lord God of Israel, 'The bowl of flour shall not be exhausted, nor shall the jar of oil be empty, until the day that the Lord sends rain on the face of the earth.' So she went and did according to the word of Elijah and she and he and her household ate for many days." I KINGS 17:14-15 (NASB)

Meditation

The woman in I Kings 17:14-15 had flour and water and was gathering sticks to make bread to prevent her and her son from dying of starvation. Flour supplies were scarce and bread was the main staple of their diet. Somehow, in a divine way, God kept their flour jar full.

We do not expect groceries to magically appear in our pantries if we haven't been to the supermarket. But have we ever wondered how we got through a particularly difficult passage or season in life? Somehow, the mortgage was paid. Despite a layoff, bills were paid by juggling balls in the air. In fact, it's often a true balancing act. We feel off-centre, trying to catch balls that are beyond our reach.

I believe in working with what we have. We can't work with what we do not possess. We might want to identify how much flour we have in our jars. The more flour we think is in our jars, the fuller the jars may appear. We have to work with the "ingredients" we possess—our character traits, skills, knowledge, education, and experiences. The more we mix our ingredients together, the more likely we will be able to generate ideas that stimulate our desires, guiding us to a path where we can make a contribution. As we meet people, interact, and search for information, new angles or ideas present themselves.

I loved the movie *Apollo 13*. The spacecraft set out on a mission to land on the moon. However, the mission was subverted and replaced with returning home safely when the astronauts began losing oxygen because of damaged tanks from an onboard explosion. The astronauts were floating without heat and were nearing death. The ground crew simulated the conditions in space, taking account of what the spacecraft did possess: duct tape, cardboard, and a myriad of floating parts. Somehow, the ground crew developed a mock device that, if replicated in space, would provide the much-needed flow of oxygen. The space crew constructed the device as instructed and were once again able to breathe oxygen. It was a step in the right direction.

Maybe we feel we are working Plan B instead of Plan A. Our original mission was aborted and now we are suspended, trying to figure out how to get back home. However, God is in the business of turning Plan B into Plan A. Maybe the results will be even more stupendous and meaningful because of the hardships we experienced.

In reality, we have to work with what we have. We have to think of the resources our minds and bodies possess. Great things can be accomplished with very little. People who have accomplished great things remember when they had next to nothing to work with. However gruelling the process may be, don't give up. My father's favourite saying was, "Don't give up!" In anxiety and depression, perseverance is often the lever of choice.

Action Step

Make a list of what you possess. What assets do you have: interests, passions, desires, experiences, education, background, contacts, networks, work experiences, accomplishments, knowledge? How do these aid you? Hang on to what you have. Employ your particular skills and gifts in whatever setting you find yourself. You might be surprised to discover what you have to work with.

Prayer

Lord, I love to be resourceful. I often forget how much I have to work with. You created the world out of nothing. Help me to mix the resources available to me and come up with new recipes for life. You have granted me talents, gifts, ideas, family, friends, and more. I can take what You have given me and make more for myself. Invigorate my mind with ideas of how to be creative with what I have.

My Journal

Winner!

Scripture

"Do you not know? Have you not heard? The Everlasting God, the Lord, the Creator of the ends of the earth, does not become weary or tired. His understanding is inscrutable. He gives strength to the weary, and to him who lacks might He increases power. Though youths grow weary and tired, and vigorous young men stumble badly, yet those who wait for the Lord will gain new strength; they will mount up with wings like eagles, they will run and not get tired, they will walk and not become weary." ISAIAH 40:28-31 (NASB)

"He who testifies to these things says, 'Yes, I am coming quickly.' Amen. Come, Lord Jesus." REVELATION 22:20 (NASB)

Meditation

I called my former colleague to say farewell; I would no longer be with the company. I wanted to explain the painful journey, but without getting a word in edgewise, he said, "We live in a fallen world, and sometimes the brokenness falls on us. But guess what? I've read the end of the book, and we win!"

Jim's words have become a famous saying among my friends. They were the perfect words for that difficult day. Jim was an active and beloved pastor for 18 years

before he came to the company. During our time as
co-workers, he and his wife were involved in a terrible
car accident on a cold wintry night while returning
from a family Christmas celebration. He'd hit black ice
on an Indiana highway, flipping his car over. Jim knew
something was terribly wrong when he was viewing his
own backside in front of him.

Unfortunately, although Jim's wife was unharmed,
Jim suffered paralysis from the waist down, having
to endure months of physical rehabilitation. Jim's
wheelchair carried him through permanent disability;
all former freedoms changed. Despite the tragedy, Jim
tells his story with a luxurious sense of humour.

While we were colleagues, I remember his grit and
determination in joining the gang in travel. Ever the
jokester, Jim wheeled onto the moving walkway in the
Chicago O'Hare airport and his wheelchair became
stuck as he was trying to exit it, causing a pile-up of
bodies and briefcases behind him. Luckily, everyone
walked away without injury, but the story has become
one of Jim's humorous tales.

My colleague was able to say that in spite of his
brokenness, he was a winner. In spite of anxiety and
depression, we are, too. We have much to fight for here
on earth and we need to remember that ultimately, we
are part of the winning team in the life to come.

We can be hit hard in this world—social phobias,
hoarding disorders, eating disorders, anxiety disorders,
depression; the DSM (Diagnostic and Statistical
Manual of Mental Disorders) of life continues. In my
online search about DSM, I found one site with the
title, "DSM Made Easy." But there is nothing easy
about any mental disorder.

"Make no mistake," said the aging John while in exile under the reign of the Emperor Domitian, "Jesus will come back for us." We will fight to overcome all sorts of neuroses in this life, but not in the life to come. We will be given a new body, yes, but also a *new mind.* Imagine a mind without anxiety, a spirit without depression, an absence of obsessive-compulsive thinking, and complete relief from mind pain! That is our destiny.

Action Step

God intends for us, someday, to be free from mind pain and mental illness. It is His divine healing we will eagerly anticipate. Until then, we can find His strength for the journey here. When your anxiety or depression is overwhelming you, focus on the life to come. Focus on what is waiting there for you.

Prayer

Lord, You are coming to set the world to rights. To bring justice to those who have been mistreated in this life. Your Word says You are coming quickly—but I'm still here. One day, I will know a time when I have no "mind pain." I can hardly imagine. Help me to anticipate Your coming. "No eye has seen, no ear has heard, and no mind has imagined what God has prepared for those who love Him" (I Corinthians 2:9, NLT). Help me to anticipate what I do not comprehend.

My Journal

Conclusion

Scripture

"Have I not commanded you? Be strong and courageous! "Do not tremble or be dismayed, for the Lord your God is with you wherever you go." JOSHUA 1:9 (NASB)

"And he who does not take his cross and follow after Me is not worthy of Me." MATTHEW 10:38 (NASB)

"Then Jesus said to His disciples, 'If anyone wishes to come after Me, he must deny himself, and take up his cross and follow Me.'" MATTHEW 16:24 (NASB)

"Brethren, I do not regard myself as having laid hold of it yet; but one thing I do: forgetting what lies behind and reaching forward to what lies ahead, I press on toward the goal for the prize of the upward call of God in Christ Jesus Christ." PHILIPPIANS 3:13-14 (NASB)

"But they were looking for a better place, a heavenly homeland. That is why God is not ashamed to be called their God, for he has prepared a city for them." HEBREWS 11:16 (NLT)

Recently, I seem to hear Jesus say to me, "Beverlee, take up your cross of 'awful feelings' and follow me.

Take up your cross of anxiety and follow me. It's your way of identifying with me." Now He seems to say the same thing every morning, asking me to take up my cross and follow Him to see what He has for me.

You can insert your name and replace the word "cross" with your word. "_____(name)_____ , take up your _____ and follow me." Maybe it's a battle with your weight, a constant drip of physical pain, a habit or behaviour you would like to change, a wretched divorce, a hateful child, an abused past, an unforgettable wrong turn in the journey of life. Take up that cross and follow His way.

I read both the book of Job and Joshua in conjunction with each other. The "J contrast"—the suffering Job and the conquering Joshua. Both were men of God, but with very different assignments.

"We may have concluded that a good and healthy life is reserved for people who are better or stronger than we are, but there is a Promised Land for each one of us. We need to be courageous. We need to believe that there can be good things in life for us. We, too, can be encouraged that regardless of our own past failures and those of our family, we can start again. We can find our way out of the chaos of the wilderness into the Promised Land of productive and healthy living. There probably have been times when we all had high hopes for a promising life before those hopes were dashed. But then, through the crazy and chaotic circumstances of growing up, we learned to settle for a life that was far less than what we had once hoped for" (*The Life Recovery Bible,* Tyndale, 1998, pg. 257).

Maybe we have left Egypt. We made the initial evacuation. We are out. But the journey to the Promised Land has just begun. We have miles to go before we sleep. We thought that if we left Egypt, it was just a hop, skip, and a jump into Canaan. But somehow, the journey leaves us longing for leaks and bricks that symbolized our time of exile in Egypt. Not unlike the Israelites in their place of slavery, we are sometimes imprisoned in our lives by destructive habits and unimaginable heartaches. This is a time to believe as Joshua and Caleb did. They believed the land they saw, although inhabited by many enemies, could become theirs: the land of Canaan, the land flowing with milk and honey.

It is very clear that God had the power to change the very perceptions of people so that their enemies would be terrified of them. This fact gripped me recently. God literally changed how others viewed the Israelites; it was very different from how they viewed themselves. That's often the problem: how we see ourselves from the inside out—we listen to the half-truths and lies we tell ourselves without entertaining the opinions others have of us. God can affect how others see us. The enemies of Israel were terrified by God's work. Isn't that amazing? He can give us favour in front of a King. *"The nations of the world are worth nothing to Him. In His eyes they count for less than nothing – mere emptiness and froth"* (Isaiah 40:17, NLT).

As the Israelites spied the land of milk and honey, the inhabitants appeared as giants and their collective sigh instituted another 40 years of circling until everyone came to believe. It's time to be strong and courageous regarding your cross. It's a time to embrace your journey of recovery and follow Christ into your Promised Land.

The Land of Oz is not the land of Uz (the biblical land where Job lived and suffered). Ours is not a journey to find a mythical Emerald City; rather, we move toward what Augustine called the City of God, that place where God's kingdom will provide for us wholeness and eternal well-being. It's a place of relief and belief; it's striving after and not shrinking back. Instead of struggling on a treacherous journey along a yellow brick road, we find ourselves moving together on the path of brokenness toward a place of ultimate wellness and recovery. We might say the journey of recovery is the way home.

God has spoken to me clearly about these things through his Word. I have been captured by the pull of God. I am resolute about moving forward, carrying my cross, and crossing over into my own recovery. I beckon to you to come along with me.

Dear Aunt Louise,

I really enjoyed talking with you at Brooks Ranch. I think there is great benefit in looking backward so we can walk forward. The things you remember as a child and the feelings you have about them are very important for your life now.

The word "anxiety" is very relevant to our family history. You have experienced it. Anxiety feels awful and is very real. You are not alone. "Nearly 19% of American adults struggle with an anxiety disorder and 5 to 8% deal with depression in a given year" (*Woman's Day*, May 6, 2008). This statistic includes Christians.

People who struggle with anxiety will feel three times as bad as someone else would when something terrible happens and it will be that much harder to handle. The trouble is, Christians use "pat answers" to those who struggle with worry. Reading your Bible and praying more does not make anxiety go away! Imagine someone you know was in a car accident, lost the use of his or her legs, and was confined to a wheelchair. Would you tell that person to pray and read the Bible? Praying and reading the Bible will help—but it will not remove the disability. Anxiety is actually a certifiable disability of mental health. In other words, it is a clinically diagnosed conditioned that affects people's ability to function. There is much evidence to show that there are genetic risk factors that make a person prone to anxiety.

Now, this doesn't mean we are *victims* of anxiety or that we can do nothing about it. Remember, God understands our "hardwiring," so this anxiety does not make us less useful to God or a "bad Christian." In fact, the very anxiety we wish would go away can actually bring us closer to God because we have to depend on him more. If a person is having what I call "catastrophic anxiety," where he or she cannot cope, then professional help and care is needed. However, if the anxiety is generalized and ongoing, then there are different ways of *thinking* that can lessen the anxiety. Our mind is our greatest asset in dealing with anxiety. *"For God has not given us a spirit of fear and timidity, but of power, love, and self-discipline." (II Timothy 1:7, NASB).*

This means that we need to change how we view situations. When our mind wants to run off the train tracks, we need to stand back and view the situation in less catastrophic terms. We need to reason with ourselves. We need to rely on our thoughts and not on our *feelings*! Feelings are an interesting gift from God. If you remember the very best times in your life, you will experience very good feelings. But feelings are not a very reliable source for what we should do. Even though we *feel* awful, we can still *do* the right things. And when we do the right things, we will feel better afterward.

Remember when I told you about the 50%, 40%, and 10% pie? A scientific study by Dr. Sonja Lyubomirsky has now proven that 50% of our happiness is related to our hardwiring, 10% to our situation or circumstances, and 40% to our thinking patterns and choices. I believe this is in line with the Bible and I will give you verses and exercises you can use. First, I want to tell you what Dr. Lyubomirsky's studies have proven about happy versus unhappy people. I think her findings are very helpful when dealing with anxiety. The following 12 "happiness activities" are taken from her book, *The How of Happiness: A Scientific Approach to Getting the Life You Want*.

Happiness Activity No. 1: Expressing Gratitude

This means counting your blessings, savouring the moment, staying present-oriented, and keeping a sense of wonder and appreciation for life. Gratitude reduces negative feelings and takes worry away. Worry and gratitude cannot exist in the mind at the same time! Aunt Louise, if you have a notebook, keep it by your Bible, and each day, write down five things for which you are thankful. You may have to think hard, especially if you are worried or having a bad day. But God cares about your happiness.

I thought these might be some of your blessings:

1. A nice apartment
2. Loving children
3. Good friends
4. Fun activities
5. Driving independence

You can continue the list.

Happiness Activity No. 2: Cultivating Optimism

This means looking at the bright side, finding the silver lining in a cloud, noticing what's right, avoiding self-blame, and thinking good thoughts about your future, even if you are 83!

My dad was an optimistic person. He always looked for the bright side; although we were poor, he had a way of cheering us up and on. I received a few "happiness genes" from Dad, but inherited all my worry genes from my mother.

Identify negative thoughts. Keep a jar for pennies; if you encounter a negative thought, put a penny in the jar. You will quickly notice how much of your thinking is negative. Then, if you'd like, take a 3x5 card and write these questions on the card:

What else could this situation or experience mean?
Can anything good come from it?
Does it present any opportunities for me?
What lessons can I learn and apply to the future?
Did I develop any strength as a result?

Thinking brighter thoughts can become a habit. The Apostle Paul says: *"Finally, brethren, whatever is true, whatever is honorable, whatever is right, whatever is pure, whatever is lovely, whatever is of good repute, if there is any excellence and if anything worthy of praise , dwell on these things" (Philippians 4:8, NASB).*

Happiness Activity No. 3: Avoiding Overthinking and Social Comparison

I think this issue is a *really* big one, particularly in the culture in which we grew up. Take note of the following quotes from Dr. Lyubomirsky's book:

"I have found that truly happy people have the capacity to distract and absorb themselves in activities that divert their energies and attention away from dark or anxious ruminations (to turn something over in the mind)."

"A notable feature of overthinking is that it draws on a person's mental resources. We found, indeed, that some of our participants tend to ruminate about bad experiences and that this overthinking harms their

~~concentration, and ultimately their performance, at~~
~~demanding everyday activities like reading and writing.~~"

"Over the next few years, we found that the happiest
people take pleasure in other people's successes and
show concern in the face of others' failures."

"No insight is gained from overthinking. To the
contrary, rumination makes things only worse."

Happiness Activity No. 4: Practising Acts of Kindness

Providing assistance or comfort to other people can
deliver a welcome distraction from your own troubles
and ruminations, as it shifts the focus from you to
somebody else.

- Give the gift of time
- Surprise someone with a home-cooked meal, a gift,
  a letter, or a phone call
- Try each week to do something that doesn't come
  naturally
- Work to develop your compassion
- Each week, do a kind deed about which you tell no
  one; expect nothing in return

Happiness Activity No. 5: Nurturing Social Relationships

I think you do this very well.

Happiness Activity No. 6: Developing Strategies for Coping

Aunt Louise, you mentioned the memory of sitting
on the porch as a little girl and wondering where your
next meal would come from. You said, "This worry has
never gone away." That threat is still very real in your

mind because it *did* happen to you. ~~Often, when we have been wounded, we feel a threat when no threat is actually present.~~ Our sense of normal has been damaged. "Some have such intense and long-lasting reactions to a trauma that they are unable to return to their previous ('normal') selves for many months or even years."

However, we can learn to cope. Often, the best way of ~~coping with anxiety is distraction.~~ In other words, doing or engaging in some activity or conversation is a better use of our time than worry. The activity has to be strong enough to distract us from our worry. I have personally found that the more I engage in others' interests and activities, the less of a habit worry becomes.

Here is a way I have learned to cope. I have chosen this phrase as my bottom line: **"Just live one more day."** Sometimes, this means just pushing through for one more hour, or just breathing.

Dump your anxiety on the Lord.

Look at the following verses. Think about them.

"Therefore, humble yourselves under the mighty hand of God, that He may exalt you at the proper time, casting all your anxiety on Him, because He cares for you. Be of sober spirit; be on the alert. Your adversary, the devil, prowls around like a roaring lion, seeking someone to devour" (I Peter 5:6-8, NASB).

"Be anxious for nothing, but in everything by prayer and supplication with thanksgiving, let your requests be made known to God. And the peace of God, which surpasses all comprehension, will guard your hearts and your minds in Christ Jesus" (Philippians 4:6-7, NASB).

"And He said to me, 'My grace is sufficient for you, for power is perfected in weakness.' Most gladly, therefore, I

will rather boast about my weaknesses, so that the power of Christ may dwell in me. Therefore, I am well content with weaknesses, with insults, with distresses, with persecutions, with difficulties, for Christ's sake; for when I am weak, then I am strong" (II Corinthians 12:9–10, NASB).

Distract yourself with another activity.

Dump your anxiety on the Lord 100 times a day, if needed.

Happiness Activity No. 7: Learning to Forgive

Forgiving doesn't mean forgetting or calling something bad, good. It doesn't mean we take away from the harm or hurt. However, it *does* mean we choose to let the person go free from our penalty—we do not poison ourselves with the poison we intend for another. We free them to God's judgment.

"Never take your own revenge, beloved, but leave room for the wrath of God, for it is written, 'Vengeance is mine, I will repay,' says the Lord." (Romans 12:19, NASB). In the Lord's Prayer, Jesus instructs us to pray, "And forgive us our debts, as we also have forgiven our debtors." Jesus goes on to say, *"For if you forgive others for their transgressions, your heavenly Father will also forgive you. But if you do not forgive others, then your Father will not forgive your transgressions" (Matthew 6:14–15, NASB).* Gulp!

Happiness Activity No. 8: Increasing Flow Experiences

In other words, do more of the things that use your gifts and talents. "Many people have the capacity to enjoy their lives even when their material conditions are lacking and even when many of their goals have not been reached. How do they do it? 1. Be open to new and different experiences (cooking, playing games, visiting a park or landmark that is new, etc.); 2. Learn until the day you die."

Happiness Activity No. 9: Savouring Life's Joys
- Relish ordinary experiences
- Savour and reminisce with family and friends
- Transport yourself through ideas and dreams of things you would like to do or places you might like to see
- Replay happy days
- Celebrate good news
- Be open to beauty and excellence
- Be mindful
- Take pleasure in the senses (what you enjoy eating, smelling, touching, hearing, seeing, etc.)

Happiness Activity No. 10: Committing to Your Goals
Pursuing goals brings greater happiness than abandoning them.

Make a list of goals you would like to accomplish this year:

1. _____

2. _____

3. _____

4. _____

5. _____

Happiness Activity No. 11: Practising Spirituality

Happiness Activity No. 12: Taking Care of Your Body

Dr. Lyubomirsky found that people who practise the above 12 "happiness activities" were, in some way, shape, or form, happy people.

Aunt Louise, anxiety is like "Old Faithful;" it will never be completely shut off. Something will trigger it at some point. However, if we have some methods for coping, we can lessen its effects.

Let's go back to my example from the first page of this letter, of the person who had a car accident and is now in a wheelchair. Will this person always be victorious and feel good about his or her condition? No. Will he or she have bad days and better days? Yes. Would we get upset with this person for struggling and trying? No. Anxiety is the same. If you ask me, anxiety is a result of biochemistry, genetics, and childhood and adult wounding. So, as you said, "I never knew life could be so difficult." Jesus said that, too, but he also said, "Be of good cheer; I have overcome the world."

Aunt Louise, Christians tend to focus on being given a new body in heaven, but we will also be given a new mind that does not worry or obsess or get all tied up in knots.

I'm studying to be a Life Coach at a university in the fall and I'm trying to finish writing a devotional book for those who struggle with anxiety. I want to help if I can. You are precious to God and to me. I hope we can talk more about the past and the future together.

Love, your niece,
Beverlee

In My Control

Serenity Prayer

"God, give us grace to accept with serenity
the things that cannot be changed,
Courage to change the things which should be changed,
and the Wisdom to distinguish the one from the other.

Living one day at a time,
Enjoying one moment at a time,
Accepting hardship as a pathway to peace,
Taking, as Jesus did, This sinful world as it is,
Not as I would have it,
Trusting that You will make all things right,
If I surrender to Your will,
So that I may be reasonably happy in this life,
And supremely happy with You forever in the next.
Amen.

Reinhold Niebuhr (1932-2000)

Old Proverb:
A person changed against his will is of the same
opinion still—*you* can only control *you.*

OUT OF MY CONTROL
I can do nothing about it

IN MY CONTROL
What I can do about me

About the Author

Beverlee Buller Keck

Beverlee grew up in the heart of the San Joaquin Valley in California, where Mennonite Brethren farmers turned the land into "the fruit basket of the nation." After university, she joined the staff of Campus Crusade for Christ and worked with students at the University of Washington, Northern California, and Great Britain. She met and married Durwin, with whom she moved to Southern California for Durwin's theological studies at Talbot School of Theology. Beverlee joined the staff of two churches as a Director of Women's Ministries and Church Resource Ministries following Talbot. During this time, she also worked as a Business Manager for her daughter, Molly, in the entertainment industry for 10 years. Her last career position was with a financial services company as a Church Relations Manager.

Beverlee is currently a cottage dweller in Orange County, California with her husband. She has one adult daughter. Beverlee loves to write, read, swim, and travel and enjoys the riches of family and friends.

If you would like to share your own personal story with Beverlee, send an email to: bev@thecovereddish.com

Retreats, Conferences, Seminars: You also can contact Beverlee at the same email address listed above for speaking engagements.

To order additional copies, please contact Kindred Productions by phone: 1.800.545.7322 or you may order online at www.kindredproductions.com